NEW BOOK FROM SPIRITUAL GUIDE
KESLEY TWEED

THE ASCENDED LIFE

THE ULTIMATE SPIRITUAL GUIDE:
WHERE LIGHTWORKERS
COME TO EVOLVE

UNLOCK YOUR SPIRITUAL GIFTS AND ASCEND FASTER
THAN YOU EVER THOUGHT POSSIBLE

THE ASCENDED LIFE

The Ultimate Spiritual Guide

Where Lightworkers Come to Evolve

KESLEY TWEED

Copyright © 2024 Kesley Tweed

All Rights Reserved

CONTENTS

INTRODUCTION: 1
  THE JOURNEY BEGINS 1
    EXPLORATION 6

CHAPTER 1 8
  WHEN LIFE DOESN'T GO AS PLANNED 8
    EXPLORATION 14

CHAPTER 2 16
  CHASING LOVE 16
    Exploration 23

CHAPTER 3 25
  MEDITATION 25
    EXPLORATION 34

CHAPTER 4 36
  BREATHE THROUGH IT 36
    EXPLORATION 44

CHAPTER 5 46
  INTUITION 46
    EXPLORATION 54

CHAPTER 6 55
CHAKRAS AND YOUR MAGIC 55
  EXPLORATION 77

CHAPTER 7 79
ASTROLOGY PART I: 79
ASCENDING WITH THE SUN, MOON AND STARS 79
  EXPLORATION 86

CHAPTER 8 87
ASTROLOGY PART II: 87

CHAPTER 9 108
RE-LEARNING LOVE 108
  EXPLORATION 114

CHAPTER 10 116
THE REBIRTH 116
  EXPLORATION 124

ABOUT THE AUTHOR 126

INTRODUCTION:

THE JOURNEY BEGINS

> "People always asked her where she was going. Without fully knowing herself, she said, 'In the right direction.'"
> —Unknown

I awoke with a jolt. Curtains, shifting on a gentle breeze filtered the moonlight that glowed off bare white walls, and shadowed an empty closet. It was another stark, rented room.

"Where am I?"

On that night, the answer to my question was Jaco, Costa Rica. My wandering disposition and nomadic lifestyle had brought me to Jaco seeking paradise on a budget.

It wasn't uncommon in those days, and in the long nights alone, for me to wake at 2 a.m.—the dreaded 2 a.m.—and struggle to remember where I was. I had been to six countries in the last seven months, and had *"lived"* in dozens of rented rooms much like this one. The only consistency was my rusty red 70-liter backpack and whatever I could fit inside of it for that leg of the journey.

Of course I would feel lost.

In hindsight, it wasn't the rented rooms at all.

Strangely, my next question was not about what had woken me. It was a bigger, deeper question. One I had been asking myself a lot lately.

"Who am I?"

It was certainly an inconvenient time for an identity crisis. This white-walled bedroom was a block from the most amazing sunsets and crystal clear blue waters I had ever witnessed. This was the destination I'd been dreaming of for years, and now I was here to live for the next two months. With an online coaching business, it was as easy as packing up my laptop and finding a Wi-Fi connection.

In fact, my dreams were coming true before my very eyes. Eight months prior, I had left my job in corporate America to pursue my passion for fitness by starting a coaching business. I had witnessed the beauty of the world in places like Thailand, India, Bali, and New Zealand. I had met new friends and discovered new interests.

I was living the vision I had created for my life -- to travel the world and help others look and feel better.

So why did I feel so uncomfortable in my own skin?

Why did life still feel like such a struggle?

Now, alone in a strange room in the middle of the night, without the sunset, without that blue water, the struggle overcame me. I wanted to crawl up the stale white walls. I wanted to claw myself out of my own skin. My own thoughts and emotions were like hands gripping my neck squeezing the life right out of me.

I had heard somewhere that when we wake up in the wee hours in the morning, it's the Universe speaking to us. Clearly, I wasn't getting it.

I begged the Universe for answers.

"Why? What do you have to tell me? What am I missing?"

For three anxiety-stricken nights in a row, the same 2 a.m. insomnia occurred. In an effort to reduce the discomfort, I would pace back and forth between the bed and my laptop on the kitchen table, where I'd try to sort through my thoughts in writing.

In hindsight, it seems so simple. I had food to eat and a relatively healthy body. I had a roof over my head and a family back home who loved me. I was doing the things I was passionate about, like traveling, learning, and helping others.

But after leaving my corporate job and big city lifestyle, I had finally slowed down enough to notice what I had been running from my entire life.

"What will they think?"

"How will they feel?"

"What would they do?"

3 THE JOURNEY BEGINS

"What am I missing?"

"What's wrong with me?"

To this day, I do not know who *"they"* are, but this imaginary group had a profound, gut-wrenching effect on me. They were my inner voice.

It was on nights like the one in Costa Rica when the physical, mental, and emotional pressure to be who I thought *"they"* thought I *"should"* became too much to bear.

Read that again.

*…**The pressure to be who I thought** "they" **thought I** "should" **be.***

"They" weren't real people, and who I thought I *"should"* be was merely an idea. One I couldn't fully understand, let alone live up to. It was an idea I had created in an attempt to fit in, avoid pain and rejection, and earn love.

No wonder I felt lost and confused.

But from that place of intense pain, confusion, and exhaustion -- the most powerful thing happened.

I decided I wasn't going to live like that anymore. I decided there had to be another way.

And it's in those moments where we decide, that magic happens.

"Choices, babe," I said to myself.

It was not the kind of instantaneous *"magical"* transformation where I saw light and heard a choir of angels. The process of healing and recreating *"me"* happened in layers—layers of deep emotional release, on my knees begging the Universe for help, followed by new insight and the type of peace and freedom that can only come from complete soul-shifting surrender.

> ***And if you're reading this, you are being called to a soul-shifting journey all your own – a journey to uncover your inner light - your ascended self!***

There's something that happens to a person's eyes once they've connected with their ascended self – it's like you can see a light that radiates from the deepest part of them. Maybe you know what I'm talking about.

We can't always see that light in ourselves, but we can feel it. It feels like freedom. It feels like comfort. It feels like empowerment and passion and purpose.

That light shows up as a human with the desire to live not only the length of life – but the depth of life. To follow her soul's calling, to handle life's challenges with gratitude and grit, and to see unlimited possibilities.

That's why I'm writing this book. I look out into the world and see millions of beautiful souls on this amazing journey called the human experience. But for so many of us – unless we've done the work to reclaim it -- there's no light in our eyes.

Somewhere along the way, we lost the connection with the eternal light that lives in us. This can happen due to pain, trauma, or simply through the process of *"growing up"* and being faced with *"real life"* responsibilities.

The *"cutting off"* from that light within is what leads us to feel lonely, empty, and uncertain. It's what causes us to reach for things outside ourselves – money, goals, relationships, substances, social media likes, what *"they"* might think -- to fill what feels like and unquenchable thirst within.

The truth is, it's not a *"void"* that needs to be filled. But a connection that needs to be rebuilt.

This book will provide you tools to reconnect you with your true self. It's not a process of reading and doing, but a process of unbecoming and becoming. It's not about completing a checklist of journal questions and learning how to meditate – but something that one day you'll feel. You'll feel that balance of freedom – and stability – of passion and inner peace.

And likely, around that same time, someone will look at you say, *"You're different. I can see it in your eyes."*

That's how you'll know you've found it – your light.

On that day, you'll step back and realize that the unquenchable thirst—the one you one thought could only be filled from outside—is replaced with a deep satisfaction. The satisfaction found in the relationship you've created with yourself.

The emptiness you once felt is replaced with a deep sense of purpose and passion for life. The uncertainty is healed by an unbreakable connection to a voice that guides you from within.

***

How to Use this Book

If you're here and picked up this book, you were born to do this work.

"The Ascended Life" is not the type of book you read, but the type of book you experience. You will not awaken your ascended self by skimming written words on a page and processing it in the same way you process information like you learned in school.

Your true self can only be found by journeying deep within **YOU**. As you'll learn throughout the book, sometimes that means looking at the *"dark"* places or doing the deep work we would rather avoid.

It's likely that your light is trapped beneath that darkness, and it is only by going through it – transforming it -- that you will find your light. Together, let's go there.

Establishing a Daily Alignment Practice

We'll use meditation and journaling as the tools for our journey. You will also be learning about supplemental tools like energy healing, intuitive development and astrology.

In order to get the full benefit from this book, it's essential to develop a *"Daily Alignment Practice."* What this means is that you make time each day to connect with you. The amount of time can vary; I recommend at least 20-30 minutes. It's important to fill your cup – connect with your heart and your soul – on a daily basis. The goal is to *"live"* in alignment with your highest self. In order to get to that place of consistency, you must build the connection with your inner truth and light on a daily basis.

Although it's not required, I highly recommend early mornings for your *"Daily Alignment Practice."* Many research studies have shown the value of morning routines and rituals in helping us set the tone for the day.

Create a ritual that nourishes you. In this book, you'll be receiving guidance for meditation, journal questions and other activities to help you re-ignite your inner light. However, you may also consider additional elements to nourish your body, mind and soul such as physical movement, stretching or yoga, breath work, and healthy food or beverages including coffee or tea.

Also consider all the senses. For example, can you add music, candles or incense, beautiful photos or art nearby, or other elements to add texture to your practice?

Since you'll be doing deep emotional work, you may need to establish a *"buffer"* between the deep, transformational time and everyday life. I like to use a more *"mental"* podcast or book, music or exercise to help me transition from my spiritual practice to *"life."*

Here are a few additional tips to guide your journey.

Start a separate journal for this experience. You will need a place to record your thoughts and emotions, which can be digital or traditional pen and paper. If you do go with a hard copy journal, pick something that you love. I find that high quality or visually appealing journals are worth the investment.

◊ Break the rules. Put perfection aside. If you enjoy writing long paragraphs in a journal, do that. If you like to type on an electronic device, go for it. If you're like me and simply scribble bullet points, that's cool, too. Highlight, underline, take notes or scribble in the margins of this book. As you read, pick out what really resonates with you. What speaks to a deeper part of you? Don't just read. Experience the words. Feel the words.

◊ Consider any unwritten rules you have about journaling that need to be released now. We've all had experiences with grammar and penmanship crazed teachers, bosses or family members. If there are any *"rules"* you have about what your journaling should be or should look like, use the question in the Exploration to release those now. Consider this the first transformation step in your journey of letting go of self-judgment.

◊ Give yourself permission to take it slow and go deep. The questions at the end of each chapter are called, *"Exploration"* because they are meant to take you to new places within yourself. Although I encourage a commitment to a daily practice, there is no timeline for this type of work. It's a journey to understanding the most important thing you will ever study: you. Take your time. It's about depth and not *"getting through"* or checking a box.

◊ Throughout this text, I use the words *"light"* and *"the Universe."* Feel free to substitute any term that resonates with you to describe the life force and the essence within you. You may choose to see it as your inner guidance system, your higher self, love, source, or consciousness. Or you may connect with a more external energy such as God, guides, angels, or a higher power. The terminology doesn't matter. Consider these are all different labels for the same indescribable, yet undeniable, force.

◊ The Exploration or what you read may pique your curiosity and start you on a search for something beyond this book. Take detours when they call you. Explore, trust your intuition, and enjoy the journey.

Let's make magic, my friend.

EXPLORATION

Use the questions below to help you prepare to get the most from this book.

1. **How do you want to feel, or what do you want to learn, by the end of this book?**

2. **Is there anything specific in life you want to change or improve?**

3. **What would it mean for you to live in alignment with your highest self?**

4. **What might a Daily Alignment Practice look like for you? (If you already have one, consider opportunities to re-energize it.)**

    a. **What time will you do it? (If mornings, do you need to set an alarm for earlier? If yes, do it now.)**

      b.   Where might you create the physical space and peaceful environment?

      c.   What activities can you add to nourish your body, mind and soul beyond meditation and journaling?

      d.   What can you incorporate into your Daily Alignment Practice to wake up your senses?

      e.   What actions do you need to take NOW to prepare for this journey?

5. Do you have any rules about what journaling "should be" that need to be released now?

"The deeper you go, the higher you'll fly."

– Deepak Chopra

CHAPTER 1

WHEN LIFE DOESN'T GO AS PLANNED

> *"There are no wrong turns, only unexpected paths."*
> —Mark Nepo

SYKESTON, NORTH DAKOTA, POPULATION 108.

I grew up on a farm in the heart of North Dakota. Being a kid was filled with the simplicity of summers spent riding our bikes along gravel roads for ice cream at the Country Café and winters of basketball games and family trips to snow ski in Montana. Although I was a small town farm girl, I was always a girl with stars in her eyes and big dreams in her heart. I would watch successful women on **TV** – from Miss America winners to Katie Couric, host of the Today Show – dreaming of the places I would go and who I would become.

I also dreamed what most girls dream. I hoped one day I would meet my Prince Charming, have a beautiful wedding and create the fairy tale life.

When I was 18 years old, I started dating the man who would be my future husband. He too was a small town farm kid, the star of the high school basketball team. We dated for five years then did what many small town kids do after graduating from college. We got married.

It took place in my hometown Catholic church on a hot summer day, surrounded by about 500 of our closest friends and family. It was a true celebration and the perfect hometown wedding I'd always dreamed of. The picture-perfect ceremony was followed by a reception and dance at a local Eagles Club, where we shut down the street to dance late into the night.

WHEN LIFE DOESN'T GO AS PLANNED

Our first two years of marriage were solid. Not perfect, but good. Stable. He loved coaching high school basketball, fantasy football and weekends spent at home on the family farm. I was working at a non-profit community center in a job I loved, training for marathons and dreaming of traveling the world. Sure, we had different goals and interests, but beyond that -- it worked.

Until it didn't.

"Kesley, we have to talk."

One evening, I walked into my living room to those words from my husband. Suddenly, my fairytale life took a turn I never saw coming – and never expected.

That conversation was the beginning of a long journey for us. We tried counseling, talking and compromising; but, things only got worse.

We stayed married, continued to live together and shared a bank account. We did everything we could to appear to have a happy marriage. Beneath the smiles and façade of a young and vibrant couple were nights spent sharing a bed, but nothing more.

The heaviness and pain I carried in my heart, radiated up to my neck and throat. There was so much I wanted to say. So much anger and blame I was carrying. So much fear. In fact, the emotional pain was so great there are very few moments from that time that I remember – and even fewer moments where I let myself feel the extent of the pain.

Over time, my light began to dim. The woman who once faced each day with a healthy dose of excitement and positivity, seemed like a distant memory. I was tired of pretending. Tired of days spent hiding in the bathroom stall at work, tears rolling down my cheeks in silence.

I felt trapped, wracked with guilt. Stuck in a marriage I knew wasn't working, yet too afraid to let go. I was paralyzed by a long list of fears.

Financial fears... Financially, I didn't see any way for me to make it on my own. We already had a mortgage **and** a rent payment due to a recent relocation for my job. There was no way to make the numbers add up to cover the cost of another monthly payment.

Fear of hurting another...Despite the challenges we went through and our differences, our vows were taken with the full intention of love that would last forever. As much it wasn't working, it still hurt to feel unloved and unloving.

Fear of never finding *"the one..."* I feared I was too old. Damaged goods. If this ended, I was sentenced to being alone for life.

Fear of who I was without him... My entire identity, from the time I was eighteen, rested on being in this partnership. How would I begin to think for myself? Support myself? All of our friends were connected. Who would stand by me?

Fear of what others would think... I was a raised in the Catholic church, and divorce was a sin. Would I burn in Hell?

I processed my pain and fear in pages upon pages of journals and many long runs and tear-filled wine nights with my girlfriends.

My parents were another saving grace during this time. I felt their love -- and I also felt their concern as the real me began to slip away. Finally, one Saturday in February 2011 after two days together with my dad and mom – these few words from my father changed the entire trajectory of my life.

"Kesley, you have become a shell of your former self."

He had described how I felt perfectly. I felt like a shell. There was no feeling, no emotion, no spark left in me. I had shut it all down in an effort to protect myself. But this statement was like a shock to my brain – a wake-up call to my soul, the first step in reconnecting to the light that still lived within me.

And so, I decided.

"Choices, babe."

That Monday, I left work on my lunch break to visit an apartment just down the road from our current residence. It was a two-bedroom with a beautiful view overlooking the hillside of Minot, North Dakota. Less than twenty-four hours later, I signed the lease on my own apartment.

Days later, I officially moved out of the apartment we shared together. As I was pulling a glass out of the cupboard, and splitting our kitchenware directly down the middle, I got a call from the realtor who was trying to sell the house that we owned together in another city – the house that had us financially strapped.

"Kesley, we have an offer!" she exclaimed.

The house we had been trying to sell for nine months—a big part of the reason I had questioned if separation was even possible—had sold.

As soon as I hung up the phone with my realtor, I burst into tears. It was like the hand of God had swooped down from the heavens to give me a giant reassuring pat on the back and say, *"Don't worry. I got you."*

I lived in that apartment for only a couple of months. I had hand-me-down furniture collected from relatives and thrift stores and only half of the belongings we once shared together. Each night, I would drift off to sleep looking out over that spectacular view over the hillside of Minot, North Dakota. I was mesmerized by the bright lights that seemed to dance upon the black hillside. My fascination with the bright lights was a sign of what was to come for the small town girl.

***

WHEN LIFE DOESN'T GO AS PLANNED

"TAKE IT IN BITES." This was the advice of colleague Larry, as we looked out over the fourth largest city in the U.S. from the 33rd floor of a high rise in downtown Houston, Texas.

As I surveyed the city and the roadways beneath us, I suddenly felt like that little girl full of big city dreams. There was a renewed sense of possibility. With my marriage on its way to dissolution, I was being given an opportunity to start again in a new city with a new job.

The six lanes of traffic I could see from the interview room as we looked out over the city scared me to death. But deep down, I knew it was the Universe calling me to my *"next right step."*

In June of 2011, I made my official move to Houston. I began to invest in a few more home-related items as I settled into the idea that this separation was likely permanent. One day, shortly after my move, I decided I needed a coffee pot. Back in the days before you could order anything you wanted online and have it arrive in less than two days, I did it the old fashioned way. I went to the store.

There I stood looking at an entire row of black coffee pots. Then, one caught my eye. It was exactly the same as the others except it was pink. **HOT PINK**.

I looked at it and immediately out of habit thought, *"No, I can't. He would hate that."*

"Wait a minute..." I thought to myself as I came to my senses. *"There is only me."*

In that moment, it all became real. I was officially alone, in a new city -- a season of my life had ended. At the same time through the purchase of a hot pink coffee pot, I realized a new season was just beginning.

In that moment, I said *"yes"* to more than the color of the machine that would make my morning cup of liquid happiness. I said *"yes"* to accepting the gift of life's unexpected turn and to embracing a bright, new beginning.

I thought back to the little girl. A little girl with big dreams. That little girl was never lost, she was there all along. But for a time I had forgotten her.

In that moment, I said *"yes"* to her, and I said *"yes"* to reconnecting with my true self.

***

Why to *"bad"* things happen?

As I write this book nearly a decade later, I've spent a lot of time reflecting on *"why."*

Why did the life I had planned not turn out the way I expected? Why did I have to go through so much pain and heartbreak? Why was the one thing I wanted most – love – so difficult? Maybe this whole thing was all my fault?

If you've ever been in a place of extreme disappointment, heartbreak, shock, or disillusionment with life -- maybe you can relate or have even asked similar questions.

For as long as I can remember, I have believed that everything, happens for a reason. So when I was faced with the biggest heartbreak of my life, I had to look deep within and ask, *"But why?"*

I went to therapy, life coaches, found a new church, and did personal development. I spent hours in meditation and journaling in order to make sense of it all.

Through all of that, I uncovered a deep truth within myself that I'll offer as a hypothesis for you to explore now. This is a truth that not everyone will accept. I can't say that it's the ultimate truth, but what I can say is that it feels as true as anything I've ever known.

The truth I uncovered is that when we think we're doing it *"wrong"* because life doesn't go as planned or something *"bad"* happens, we are actually doing it *"right."* *"Right"* as in – that's the way it's supposed to be.

I realized life isn't supposed to be perfect. We aren't supposed to be perfect. We are here to learn. To grow. To evolve. To help one another as we navigate this journey of life.

They teach us all kinds of knowledge in school. Those who raise us do an amazing job preparing us for life. But there are some things that can't be taught – they can only be learned through experience. There are also some parts of your journey that are unique to you – lessons that become gifts when we choose to see beyond our human pain.

The most painful moments of my life thus far led me to the greatest gifts I could ever receive. Through that divorce, I learned how strong I really am and who I really am. I saw all the ways I wasn't honoring my true self – my hopes, dreams and uniqueness -- and how the Universe was providing me with an opportunity for a course correction.

I learned to move through fear and trust the Universe and my own inner voice. I created a new definition of love and learned how precious true intimate connection is.

I learned that we are here to grow -- and to give. If we don't grow, at some point we won't have any more to give. Therefore, I learned to place my focus on growth – instead of perfection.

Consider that we are more than a human mind and body. Within us there is a light— the kind of energy that is eternal. Some might call it a soul. For our soul to evolve, it requires that we go through what our human mind tells us is failure, heartbreak, loss and disappointment. Personally, I like to think of it as *"earth school."*

For me, living out my evolutionary journey and part of my earth school certificate in *"rolling with the punches."* meant giving up the dream of the happily ever after and white picket fence in exchange for a bright city lights, skyscrapers and a hot pink coffee pot.

And I wouldn't change it. The greatest gifts I've ever received came from the very thing I once saw as gut-wrenching, heartbreaking pain.

I bet that if you look at your life you can also see how maybe it hasn't turned out exactly as you had thought. There were seasons where you thought it wasn't as it *"should be"*– and it hurt. And I bet if you look more deeply you can see, hidden beneath the pain, a gift. It's waiting to be claimed. Have you chosen to receive it?

Receiving the gift

What stops us from receiving the gift -- the soul lesson and the opportunity to reclaim our light? In a word – fear. We hold on to what feels safe. To what we know. We want to avoid the pain of going deeper or making choices that feel uncomfortable.

But if we are to advance on our journey – to get the most from this human experience, we must learn the art of letting go. Gracefully releasing the pain of the past and creating space for new energy to come into our life.

This is exactly what happened in my life when I took that step to move out, despite an uncertain future, and the Universe opened a door for me. I like to say, the Universe always meets us halfway.

Sometimes the release is physical – moving, letting go of belongings, jobs, relationships, etc. But it's also emotional, spiritual and mental. Releasing requires developing new beliefs and sometimes a new identity.

As we seek to understand this idea of *"letting go"* and how endings and new beginnings are ultimately one in the same, let's look at something that's more familiar to all of us. Nature. I like to see the cycles we go through as humans as a reflection of the seasons. Think of your life as a constant progression of spring, summer, winter and fall.

- Spring: A time of new beginnings, new energy, new goals and intentions where seeds are planted to harvest later.
- Summer: A time of tremendous growth when the seeds begin to take shape. Summer is filled with light and very little darkness.
- Fall: A time of harvest, when the benefits of our hard work and patience pay off. We *"harvest"* the rewards and celebrate our efforts reaching their peak.
- Winter: A time of increased darkness. A time when we let go of the previous cycle, turn inward and create space for a new cycle to occur.

And just when we think winter will last forever – spring comes again. It always does.

So where are you now, in your life? What cycle are you in? Have you been stuck in winter for way too long, going through the motions of life, but not really living? If so, what needs to be released?

Are you in spring or summer, planting and tending to your goals and intentions? If so, how can you make the most of and truly appreciate this season of such beauty?

Are you in fall reaping the benefits, celebrating the rewards?

Think for a second about the light that exists in this knowing. You – the ascended being that you are – are on a continuous cycle of evolution. There is so much power in that. Sometimes it takes us stepping back from seeing life from a micro perspective and taking a higher point of view – seeing it through superhuman eyes, a birds eye view. Soul perspective.

When times get dark, when winter sets in remember everything – **EVERYTHING** – happens for a reason. Spring is just around the corner.

It's all part of your unique magical adventure called life.

EXPLORATION

1. **What season of life are you in now?**

    a. **Spring**: A time of new beginnings, new energy, new goals and intentions where seeds are planted to harvest later.

    b. **Summer**: A time of tremendous growth when the seeds begin to take shape. Summer is filled with light and very little darkness.

    c. **Fall**: A time of harvest, when the benefits of our hard work and patience pay off. We "harvest" the rewards and celebrate our efforts reaching their peak.

    d. **Winter**: A time of increased darkness. A time when we let go of the previous cycle, turn inward and create space for a new cycle to occur.

2. **How might you make the most of this season?**

    a. **If "winter," know that it too serves a purpose. What might the purpose of your "winter" be? How will you know when it is time to move forward into a new beginning?**

3. **In what ways has life surprised you or turned out differently than you thought it would?**

4. **What challenges and emotions did these experiences bring up in you?**

5. **How did these experiences change you?**

6. What gifts did you receive from the experience?

"Every season is one of becoming, but not always one of blooming. Be gracious with your ever-evolving self."

— B. Oakman

CHAPTER 2

CHASING LOVE

> *"No one can dim the light that shines from within."*
> *—Maya Angelou*

My new season and new zip code brought a completely different environment and lots of big goals. I quickly made friends, began to travel solo and climbed the corporate ladder.

In fact, I didn't stop. I detested anything that resembled sitting still. Naps. **TV**. Being stuck in the same job too long without a promotion.

I was a #goalgetter in every sense of the hashtag and honestly, have been for as long as I can remember. In high school it showed up as an obsession with straight As, countless hours shooting free throws in my barn to be the best basketball player I could possibly be, and a *"nice to everyone"* attitude that resulted in attending what may be a record number of proms. And to be honest, this persona served me. There were very few goals I did not achieve.

Whenever times get tough – brighter days are just a goal-setting session away. So naturally, a short time after my divorce, I made a list of 100 goals I wanted to achieve. It was an exercise from a Law of Attraction book. I spent hours visualizing and creating these goals.

A couple of years later, I tallied up the list. 44 out of 100. The list included things like reaching a manager level in my job, finishing my Masters of Business Administration, traveling to Europe, and get a tattoo. My success-driven, achievement-oriented Capricorn moon was pretty satisfied at the time.

However, one goal that I had not yet accomplished seemed to jump off the page.

"To truly love and accept myself."

That one made me pause. *"What would it take to truly love and accept myself?"* Although things were going well in my life, I was moving up in my job, had a great group of friends, was traveling, and was financially stable – this seemed like quite a stretch.

I had rules about what it would take to love myself. For example, in order to love myself, someone else needed to love me – like forever – like a soul mate. If not that, then at a minimum, I must love me. Loving me meant loving the one thing I had always hated about myself. My body.

Yes, I used the word hate, and I do not use that word lightly. It pains me now, but the feeling I had for the amazing body that I now see as my temple was nothing short of hatred.

The only thing that's caused me more tears than romantic relationships is my relationship with my body. Of all the things I hated the most, getting dressed was the worst part. *"They"* - the imaginary yet loud - internal chorus of haters - would chime in with their own self-defeating chatter.

"You're fat. You've always been fat. You'll always be fat. You eat too much. Why are you so much bigger? Big boned. Stocky. Husky. Flawed!"

With an unmet goal staring me in the face, I decided.

"Choices, babe."

***

I wasn't sure where to start. After 30 years of struggling to accept my body, I thought I had tried it all. Marathon running, CrossFit, spin class, Weightwatchers. Nothing seemed to budge my idea that I was *"fat."*

My friend Allison had told me about a new gym she'd tried just down the street from my apartment in Houston, so I thought I'd give it a try, even though I fully expected to add it to the list of fitness pursuits that came up short.

On a rainy Saturday afternoon in late November, I walked through the doors of Washington Gym in Houston, Texas, for the first time. One of the owners, James, greeted me at the front door with a reassuring confidence that made me question my own self-doubt. He guaranteed results. *"Nothing to lose, except those 10-20 pounds that are the distance between me and my own happiness"* I thought.

On January 2, 2016, I started my journey with Washington Gym. I learned how to squat and deadlift and do pull-ups. But it was about so much more than lifting weights. When I had a barbell on my back, I felt strong and empowered. The day I completed my first chin-up is one of the proudest moments of my adult life.

After six months, I was in the best shape of my life. In true achiever fashion, I found myself asking, *"What's next?"* When my coach suggested a fitness competition, I slept on it for a couple of nights and after three days, I announced to James that I was in.

And so it began – months of lugging around plastic containers of chicken and broccoli and doing fasted cardio. For the most part, I loved training. I felt strong, empowered and I was seeing consistent results. As the body fat percentage got lower and lower, in my mind I was slowly earning the right to love myself.

Finally, show day arrived. I packed up my platform shoes, bikinis decked out in sequins, pearls and feathers, got my spray tan, and I was ready.

After two rounds, and a long day, the moment of the awards finally came. I stood, arrayed with ten other women in my category as we struck our best poses for the final selection. My heart skipped a beat as they walked by me to award the third place metal. Not me. Second place, skipped again.

"Could it be? Could I be the winner?"

"First place goes to Kesley Tweed!" A cheer went out from my friends and family in the audience. I had won! I accepted my trophy and crown.

And suddenly, I found myself wanting more.

In this competition, the judges can opt to grant a *"pro card,"* an indication of professional status, to the first place winner in each category. I waited with hope, but they just snapped a couple of quick photos and ushered us off the stage.

No pro card.

I changed out of my pastel pink bikini and packed up my things, trying not to show my disappointment to the other contestants. Prior to this day, I had no desire, no goal of receiving a pro card. In fact, it had never even crossed my mind until I saw that others had received theirs that day.

I exited the dressing room and entered the main auditorium to greet my cheering section. I politely hugged my parents and the first few friends who made their way to me. Then I went right for my coach. Before he could even hug me or offer a congratulations, I spouted out with my finger in the air, and the opposite hand on my hip, *"I'm going to get that pro card!"*

It wasn't a proclamation of a determination, but a proclamation of desperation.

I had surpassed my wildest dreams for building a strong and beautiful body, but I still wasn't happy.

So I decided. I had to work harder.

"Choices, babe."

A short time later I started training for my second competition. For several months, I continued to get leaner and leaner – and more and more exhausted.

CHASING LOVE

Eventually my results began to stall. So I worked out harder. I made the decision – no rest days. I trained twice a day, seven days a week, which my coach was not aware of.

Meanwhile, I had decided that this whole fitness thing was more than just a passion. I wanted to make it a profession. In addition to training twice per day and working a full-time management job in the oil and gas industry, I also decided to pursue a new career as a fitness coach.

I signed up for a fitness business retreat in Asheville, North Carolina. Although I was excited to begin this new journey, a part of me was anxious about an entire weekend where so much felt out of my control. Would I be able to get my proper meals in? Would I be able to get my two sessions of training in? What would happen to my results?

The day prior to the retreat, I was at a local fitness center in Asheville, getting in my last solid workout before the weekend seminar began.

I bent down to pick up the bar for my favorite exercise – the deadlift. As I had hundreds of times before, I wrapped my fingers around the cold iron of the bar. I began to fire the muscles in my legs. The 45 pound plates didn't budge from the ground beneath them. I tried again.

This time, my grip failed, and in that moment, my soul quietly whispered, *"That's enough."*

My coach required me to take three days off from training and increase my carbohydrate intake. Rest days and carbs were rare in those days. And giving myself permission to *"indulge"* was an inner battle. I did the best I could to enjoy, including the big red apple I bought myself as a *"treat."*

I spent the time that weekend I normally would have spent at the gym journaling and meditating. The deadlift failure felt like so much more than just a failure of my body. It was a clear message from the Universe.

But what did it all mean?

What was I really looking for?

"Why?" I asked. *"Why was I doing all of this?"*

The answer to my question rose up from deep within, reminding me of the goal I had set almost two years prior. *"To love and accept myself."* It was clear the way I was going about it -- earning my own love through the pursuit of perfection -- was no longer working. In fact, if I kept this up, it might literally drive me to starvation – or insanity.

And in the quiet, in my pain and exhaustion, I decided. I decided there had to be more to life than this.

"Choices, babe."

***

What's your "why?"

That day at gym was the first of many messages and wake-up calls from the Universe. All this effort -- striving, achieving and chasing – I kept reaching for things outside myself. When those things didn't fill me up, I reached for more.

It was exhausting. The harder I worked, the closer I should have been to my goal – right? So why did it feel like I was *"achieving"* the opposite result?

If you look closely and get really honest, maybe you can see the parallels in your own life. Maybe you've put all your focus and energy into career success, a physical or academic goal, having nice things, even investing in relationships – hoping for a positive, long-lasting result. None of these pursuits are in vain or wrong. But do we ever really feel like we have enough?

It led me to wonder, are we really looking in the right place, investing our energy into the right things?

We have eyes that see an external, physical reality. And again, this approach serves us in getting us to where we want to go, but is it really helping us to feel what we want to feel? Are we falling for an illusion, distracted by shiny objects?

Maybe it's time to *"see"* in a new way?

When I stepped back what I saw was that all those hours spent busting my ass in the gym, obsessing about my body were never about the *"pro card"* or a trophy or Instagram likes. It all started because I was looking to **FEEL** something. I wanted to feel enough, accepted and **LOVED**.

In fact, I think we're all looking to feel something.

I use the word *"love"* because to me that is a core human need that encompasses so much of the *"good vibes"* we seek. You may have a different emotion or name that you call what it is that you want to feel. Maybe it's freedom, peace, happiness or something else.

Whatever you call it, the outcome is the same. The *"outside in"* approach will never allow us to feel completely full – and whole – within.

When I learned to *"see,"* I woke up and realized that I been building my emotional well-being -- my source of love -- on a faulty foundation, an unreliable source. When we look outside of ourselves, we will merely have enough to survive. We'll constantly be on the search for more. It's a hunger that can never be fulfilled. It's no fault to others or the world, it's simply that the only person or thing that's with you 100 percent of the time is **YOU**.

Relying on things outside of us to fill us up inside is like hanging out behind your favorite restaurant waiting for them to throw out the scraps. You, my friend, are worthy of the seven-course meal and the best bottle of wine in the cellar. No more dumpster diving for you!

How to become a creator

My body and marriage failing ultimately led me to an awareness that was nothing short of magic.

In time I learned that if I wanted a reliable source for feeling love, happiness, freedom – all the good things I wanted to feel -- I was going to have to find a way to create it from within.

As part of my daily practice and part of my journey to self-love, I started asking myself one critical question daily.

"How do I want to feel?"

Answering this question may take some practice, but it's critical to get clear, claim and create how you want to feel. Let's face it, as amazing as life is, you would need to live millions of lives for the stars to perfectly align at a time where everything in life is perfect – you, your relationships, your paycheck, the environment, the weather, politics, etc.

It's time to step into your highest self and the powerful creator that you are by becoming a transformer of energy instead of adjusting to the energy around you like a little sponge, absorbing whatever life throws at you.

EMOTIONAL ASCENSION DAILY RITUAL

- Incorporate these steps into your *"Daily Alignment Practice"* and watch yourself transform from energy sponge to energy creator.
- Say it: Ask yourself how you want to feel. Then claim it using an affirmation. *"I AM"* is the most powerful phrase in the English language. Repeating an affirmation, *"I am,"* followed by what it is you want to feel in time reprograms your subconscious mind.
- See it: See yourself living it. Picture images that allow you to feel the emotion within you as if it already is a part of you. This can include scenes from the past, scenes you anticipate during the upcoming day, or something completely fantastical or in the future.
- Feel it: This one takes a little practice, but it's the most transformative component. What does the emotion –feel like in your body? Learn to create this emotion on demand as a set point, almost like you'd program a thermostat.
- Repeat it: Repeat this process several times until you feel the emotion you want to feel within every part of you. Repeat this process day after day until generating the emotion and the energy becomes natural.
- Believe it: In time, repetition will help this grow from simply something you say and do daily -- to a core value that is part of your essence. When we build the internal belief, that is when we are truly reconnected with our light.

Believe it

The last step, *"believe it"* is a critical part of our journey here in *"earth school."* There are various types of beliefs that can keep us stuck, limited in our perceptions and emotionally unstable.

> **Beliefs about who you are.**
>
> *Examples include:* I am not enough. I am unworthy. I will never be loved. I'm not good enough. I'm not happy person. I am fat.
>
> **Beliefs about how other people are.**
>
> *Examples include:* All men/women will hurt me. My boss is a jerk. My husband/wife never listens. People are mean and selfish. You can't trust anyone.
>
> **Beliefs about how life is.**
>
> *Examples include:* Life is hard. Love hurts. Money is the root of all evil. Money is the root of all happiness. The world is a cruel place.

If you're having a difficult time fully aligning with an emotion, it's time to check your beliefs. Many times the things we want to feel most, we want because we've spent a lifetime struggling to feel it. Transforming the old, outdated beliefs and past pain associated with them is a critical part of your ascension journey!

What do I mean by transforming beliefs?

Everything in life is perception. Imagine you and your best friend are out shopping. You stop in your tracks to admire a beautiful, red silk top. You can just 'see' yourself wearing it to the party you have coming up this weekend. Noticing your mesmerized look, your friend says, *"Oh wow. I totally agree. That is the ugliest orange top I've ever seen. Mmmm...tacky."*

"What?" you exclaim in disbelief of her comment. *"It's beautiful, bold and elegant! And it's poppy red by the way (not orange), and poppy* **RED** *happens to be the hottest color of the season in case you hadn't heard."*

How is it possible that two people could see the exact same piece of clothing and have two completely different reactions to it?

Perspective.

Shifting our perspective is like magic. You see, we think we are seeing something in our lives – our beliefs about ourselves, another, or life – as something definitive. *"It is what it is."*

But what it if it's not? What if you could actually train your brain to see it differently, making you a creator of your reality. That's exactly what I'm talking about here.

To get there, to be connected to our inner light, we must take an honest and vulnerable look at what limits us. Know that this is deeply healing and rewarding work. Be patient with yourself as you dive into updating old beliefs and patterns. It takes time, practice, repetition, courage and tenacity to let go and recreate the way that you've seen yourself and the world for as long as you can remember.

In the Exploration section, I've provided questions to help guide you in identifying and transforming limiting beliefs. You'll be learning more tools to help you with this deep healing work.

Another way that we may identify limiting beliefs is through our patterns. For example, do you keep running into the same external block over and over again? My body image struggles and patterns in relationships were indicators to me that I had internal beliefs that were resulting in external conflict. Again, so many times, we focus on *"fixing"* or changing the outside when it's really the inside that we need to transform. When we do the inner work, the external must shift to align.

So who are you?

All the magic, all the love, all the things we seek outside of us, we already are and have within. Everything you want to be and feel – you already are. If you have a desire or a wish inside of you, it's possible. Now it's time to claim who you are and what you want to feel – again, and again and again.

There is no one else like you. And there is no one else who can have the unique impact on the planet that you can have, if you choose to live authentically, boldly, wildly, and uniquely you. This is to live the ascended life! Let's claim that now.

EXPLORATION

1. What's one thing that has been a lifelong struggle, pursuit, or repeating challenge for you? Something you've always wanted but could never seem to get it – or get enough of it?

2. Why do you want it? What are you looking to feel? If you struggle with naming your emotions, try a google search for "positive emotions."

3. Use the process to anchor this emotion daily:

    a. **Say it**

    b. **See it**

    c. **Feel it**

    d. **Repeat it**

    e. **Believe it**

4. Are there beliefs that stop you from believing that you already have or are this emotion or way of being?

5. Prompts to explore limiting beliefs:

    a. My limiting belief is...

    b. The story I told myself around this belief was...(What are the 'reasons' or 'evidence' you previously used to justify this belief?)

    c. I choose to release this now because...(How is it causing you pain in your current life?)

    d. A new belief I will choose instead is...

    e. Why is it critical to choose new belief? How will it serve me?

    f. The reasons I believe this are...(Find evidence in your own life of WHY you believe this.)

"Don't adapt to the energy in the room.

Influence the energy in the room"

— *Unknown*

CHAPTER 3

MEDITATION

> *"Quiet the mind, and the soul will speak."*
> —Ma Jaya Sati Bhagavati

The months leading up to that *"deadlift failure"* at the gym were not exactly, *"normal"* by my previous definition. Three months earlier, I had attended my first personal development event. I walked on hot coals, shouted *"yes"* at the top of my lungs and ran on adrenaline and just a few hours of sleep per night. But the highlight of the event for me was, of course, goal setting. Yes, another goal. But this one was different.

At that event, I learned a lot of new theories about why we do what we do and what stops us. I transformed limiting beliefs – and for the first time ever – believed that I could do anything I decided to do.

I decided that for me, my lifelong passion for fitness must become more than just a hobby. I wanted to have a life that meant something – to help change their lives in the way Washington Gym had changed mine. I wrote down in my seminar workbook. *"I, Kesley Tweed, will leave my corporate job in February 2017 to work in fitness."*

There were very few people who knew about this deep intention and *"reach for the stars"* goal.

But I had decided. I went to work.

"Choices, babe."

I began educating myself, working on a business plan and allowing my heart to guide me. I traded in wild Saturday nights of shots and dancing well past midnight for long walks alone and listening to personal growth podcasts.

The quieter I became, the more I began to hear.

***

The first time I really *"heard"* the voice within, I was on a walk on the Buffalo Bayou in Houston, Texas. Although it was a quiet Sunday morning, I was having an internal debate. I had elected not to attend church that Sunday. I carried a deep guilt whenever I did not attend. That day, it was as if my soul was splitting in two. I could feel an old part of me saying, *"You must go. That's what good people do."*

I heard another voice -- a whisper -- but the energetic force that came with it was undeniable.

"Build your faith from the ground up."

Those specific words are etched in my memory. I had always associated the word *"faith"* with religion, with being a Christian, following the Bible and the Ten Commandments. I was baptized and raised in the Catholic Church, and it provided me with a structured spiritual practice, a community and a foundation of morals and ethics. It helped me root into an unshakeable belief in a powerful force of creation that I knew to be God.

I had decided not to go to church that morning because I felt a deep pull to connect with God in a new way. On this walk, as if out of nowhere, the doors to a new view of spirituality swung wide open. When I returned from the walk, I spent the next few hours researching everything I could find about world religions. From there, I was led to practices like chakras, energy healing and working with crystals.

But this was about more than research. That walk, that voice, was an opening -- a call to wake up. It was a call to honor the voice within me, build a personal relationship with a higher power, and forge my own unique path to ascension.

***

MEDITATION

Around that same time, my fitness coach suggested I try meditation so that I could improve my results in the gym. There was, once again, an old part of me that resisted. Meditation was the furthest thing from my go-getter *"nature."* However, there are thousands of studies out there that emphasize the benefits of meditation for improved health and mental clarity, and I was willing to do anything to win.

So, I compromised and started small by using a meditation app while doing yoga poses or holding the handrail while walking slowly with my eyes closed on the treadmill. The app was helpful in allowing me to unwind and slow my mind. In just a short time, I started to see benefits beyond the gym. I was able to better process my thoughts at work, my high blood pressure started to normalize, and overall I felt less anxious.

After a few months using the app, my friend Sharon, suggested a form of meditation called Transcendental Meditation or **"TM."** The introductory class was a significant financial investment, but the voice inside, though still faint at the time said, *"Say yes."*

And so I decided.

"Choices, babe."

On September 3, 2016, I started my meditation journey with **TM**. As part of the **TM** training, students undergo an initiation ceremony followed by an instructor-led meditation. I had high hopes for what this experience would be like. Would I hear God, see grand visions of my future, prisms of light, or be transported to an alternate reality?

The experience itself was…normal? At least compared to these glorious expectations I had. Throughout the twenty minutes, I could hear the sounds of the world around me—cars driving, sirens, birds. It seemed like I was just sitting in a chair with my eyes closed, breathing and repeating a mantra.

"How was it, Kesley?" my mediation teacher asked as we wrapped up the 20-minute session.

"I feel…" I paused to get clear on what I was feeling. It was like a small bubble of emotion at this point that I felt in the pit of my stomach – but it was ready to pop.

"ANGRY,*"* I said, shocked as it came out of my mouth. It was unlike me to be so transparent about my feelings, and anger was not an emotion I was comfortable with. I wasn't angry with anything or anyone – it was just a burning sensation deep within my belly.

She looked at me, head gently tilted to one side and said slowly and calmly, *"I think you went really deep. You should probably stay in here for a few minutes."* The moment she left the room, my emotions overcame me.

I lay on the floor in a fetal position and cried for what felt like hours. It felt like I was detoxing all of the un-cried tears stemming from my painful divorce – the fear, sadness, shame and guilt – that I had done anything to avoid feeling. The tears didn't feel painful necessarily. It felt like an emotional purge of energy. The more tears I cried, the better I felt. Finally, a half of box of tissues later, I was exhausted. But lighter. I had shed a weight I had been carrying for so long.

I committed to doing the meditation practice twice daily. After each meditation I felt a little better, a little lighter, and certainly more clear. As the ball of emotions in the pit of my stomach began to unravel, I was starting to build a stronger connection to the inner voice deep within. This wasn't easy work, but I knew it was exactly what I needed.

And so. I decided.

"Choices, babe."

I continued to stay committed to my practice – and have to this very day. Meditation has brought me more than I ever could have asked. The anxiety I once thought was just a normal part of life is gone. The ball of emotions I referenced, dismantled. The way I used to feel like a row boat in the middle of a dark and choppy ocean has been replaced with an internal sense of peace that is not always there – but I know how to get there.

Meditation truly is ascension.

***

Why meditate? (And other common questions)

The list of reasons one might choose to meditate is long and highly supported by research. I one hundred percent believe that meditation can change the world. Here are the benefits that meditation has provided for me, and a quick Google search can yield additional support for any of the benefits listed below.

1. **Mental and physical health**
2. **Emotional healing**
3. **Self-confidence and empowerment**
4. **Authenticity and self-discovery**
5. **Clarity on the big picture and everyday life**
6. **Connection to a higher power and humanity**
7. **Compassion for yourself and others**

For me, meditation is the medicine, the soul food I had been yearning for my entire life. It allowed me to make sense of this crazy, amazing journey called life.

If you ask me what I do to solve any of my biggest problems, nine times out of ten my answer will be – I meditate. In meditation, problems seem to become more permeable – transformable. Solutions seem to come out of nowhere. When I ask, the answers always come, even if they don't come in the first sitting. Sometimes, *"life"* speaks its own language and brings answers later. With patience, and quiet, the soul truly does speak.

Imagine having all the answers to life's deepest questions inside of you. You never have to go to a course, a book, Google, YouTube or ask other people what you *"should"* do? Certainly, I still collect information from a variety of resources and perspectives – but in the end, I always assimilate it through my meditation and journaling process.

Also, as you saw in my first meditation experience above, mediation has a way of dissolving and transforming long-held emotional issues.

I view meditation as an opportunity to take a time-out from our material reality and tune into the quiet voice within. It's also an opportunity to align our emotional center and become a creator of energy, as we discussed in the last chapter. Meditation puts us in a place of empowerment, to choose how we want to respond to life.

WHAT IS MEDITATION, EXACTLY?

If you look up *"meditation,"* the definition you will find is likely something along the lines of breath combined with a single point of focus. This might bring up an image of a blissed out monk or yogi on a mountain top, legs crossed in a lotus position *"om-ing."*

As lovely as this sounds, when I first heard about meditation it sounded to me like it was something for *"other people."* Like, calm people. That was certainly **NOT** me.

I've realized meditation can be for all of us – especially those with Type A tendencies. Whether you want love, peace, passion, freedom, clarity, confidence, or something else – meditation has all of this to offer and so much more.

Over time, I'm created my own definition of meditation. Meditation is shifting our awareness from external to internal through breath and intentional focus.

So the first thing I like to tell people when we begin to discuss meditation is, it doesn't have to be what you think it is. It can be any way that you nourish you, from within. Nature walks, art, music, dancing, working, making love – I believe meditation can be all of these things. It's the way we approach it as opposed to the activity itself.

I'm not looking to provide a rigid checklist of what to do and what not to do. I don't subscribe to a particular style, but I can share what I've learned through thousands of hours in my own practice, in hopes that it will encourage you and provide support as you begin to build your own meditation practice. In this chapter and the following chapter, I will continue to answer some of the most frequently asked questions I've received, to the best of my knowledge and experience, to help you get started or progress on your meditation journey.

Do I have to be still with my eyes closed to meditate?

Meditation can be done journaling, walking, stretching, doing yoga, dancing, painting, even staring at a wall. Honestly, doing anything that allows you to turn inward and focus on your inner being – your magic – versus a reaction to the external. *"Meditation"* and whatever that means for you will fill you up from the inside, creating a stronger body, mind and soul to serve your journey and others outside of meditation. Again, it's about who we become, not the process itself.

I did realize in time that one of the reasons I resisted *"stillness"* was because there was something inside of me that was very uncomfortable with not being *"productive."* I was also terrified to feel. If this is you, you are not alone. This is a topic we will explore more deeply in the next chapter.

Do I need to try to have no thoughts?

Common meditation practices provide a mantra, focus on the breath or encourage the emptying of thoughts. Although this may be ideal for some, what I can tell you is that the longest I've ever gone with no thoughts is (maybe) a couple of minutes. I really don't feel that is essential to receive deep, long-lasting, soul-opening benefits from your meditation practice. In fact, I think if we are to change the world through meditation in the way that I see is possible – we have to change the way we think about it and allow a more expansive definition.

Going back to the idea that the key is shifting our focus from external to internal, being intentional with our focus, and using the breath as an anchor in the practice. I'll tell you exactly how to do that later in this chapter.

What do I mean by intentional? It does not mean chase thoughts or emotions away like they're a pesky mosquito. When we're intentional about our focus and intentional about the thoughts we want to welcome in, we create an opportunity to observe what we are thinking and feeling from a different point of view.

It may help to write a list of potential distractions before you sit down to meditate. For example, if you have a lot to do that day, write your to-do list prior to meditation – or even the night before. Then, as part of the intentional inward focus as you begin your practice, remind yourself why this is so important. Remind yourself of how you **WANT** to feel. Say a prayer or set the intention to allow only thoughts that serve your highest good, even if they are uncomfortable.

As we'll discover later in the book, emotions and thoughts that come in meditation are likely your intuition speaking to you – shining a light on something that needs to be further explored for your highest good. If a repeated thought or deep emotion comes in, welcome it and observe.

How to start your own Ascended Life Meditation practice

So with some of the likely questions answered, you're ready for the journey of meditation. I say *"journey"* because over time your practice may evolve as you transform from the inside, out.

We will review a step-by-step approach for getting started below as a foundation as you experiment with the additional meditation styles provided throughout this book. There is a guided version of the meditation process introduced below on my website, kesleytweed.com as well as additional meditation resources. Use the guided meditation for as long as you would like, or practice on your own.

You are Magic Meditation Process

Step 1: Intentional inward focus

Close your eyes. Take one giant inhale and exhale and make a silent commitment to being present in the moment. This can be a mantra like, *"I am present," "Be here now,"* or something fun like, *"Me time," "Let that shit go," "Choices, babe. I choose me."*

Music, incense, sage or holding a crystal can also be a great way to engage the senses and cue your system that focus is shifting from external to the internal. The type of music you choose is very important. It doesn't have to be traditional meditation music. It can be anything that aligns with the mood that you'd like to set. I've meditated to everything from country to 80s rock to the sound of rain.

If you are choosing to do your meditation walking or with another activity like yoga, you can open your eyes after this first step. The *"how"* is not nearly as important as being intentional about letting go of the external and being present in the moment.

Step 2: Breath

Breathe slowly and deeply. Think of putting your breath in slow motion. Breathe down into the lowest part of your belly, allowing the midsection to gently expand as you inhale and gently contract as you exhale. This is called belly breathing or diaphragmatic breathing. Many of us have been trained to breathe into our chest, to *"suck it in"* or for a variety of reasons. However, chest breathing overuses the muscles of the chest and neck, keeps us from full oxygen exchange and elevates blood pressure and your body's stress response – leaving you fatigued and anxious. Belly breathing takes us out of the *"fight or flight"* response of the sympathetic nervous system and into the *"rest and relax"* response of the parasympathetic nervous system.

Observe how it feels to inhale and exhale. Imagine the breath as a stream of golden light. Imagine that this light is clearing and cleansing the entire body, lighting up every cell. On the exhale, you can visualize releasing cloudy, gray matter. This intentional breathing is the *"glue"* that holds your practice together. After you've established the breath, release your focus on it and allow the body to continue the rhythm naturally. This may take practice, but in time, you will not have to think about it.

Step 3: Relaxed body (intentional release of muscles)

Breath combined with relaxation of key points in the body is an instant shift. Release these key stress points by bringing your intention there and then physically releasing your muscles. You can also imagine the golden light reaching these areas as you breathe.

- Forehead
- Corners of eyes
- Jaw
- Neck and shoulders (drop the shoulders down and back, away from the ears and open through the chest)
- Base of the spine and hips

Step 4: Intentional thought

There are many models of where to direct your thoughts during meditation. I'm going to teach you the practice that I feel has yielded me the most benefit in my daily life to align me with my truth and prepare me for the day ahead. *"Intentional thought"* can take different forms, based on the experience you wish to inspire.

After you've completed steps one through three, set your intention for your day. You may use the questions we learned in the previous chapter to guide you in setting an intention, or focus, for your day.

Use the steps you learned in the last chapter to anchor your intention.

- Say it: Repeating an affirmation, *"I am,"* followed by your intention
- See it: See yourself living it.
- Feel it: Feel the emotion in your body.
- Repeat it: Repeat this process several times until you feel the emotion.

Once you feel aligned with your intention, the practice is complete. Prior to coming out of meditation, come back to your breath. Once again see the stream of golden light. Feel the inhale and exhale. Start to wiggle your fingers and toes, and when you are ready, you can open your eyes. I like to close with my hands together at the center of my chest in a prayer like position. You can seal your practice with a phrase like, *"Amen," "Namaste, the light in me honors the light in you." "I love you, thank you," "So it is,"* or the words of your choosing.

Ascension Mantras

After coaching hundreds of people through their first meditation experiences, I've come to realize the barrier to meditation is rarely knowledge. You can find a million apps, meditations, and other resources out there including a free video series and guided meditations available on my website that can teach you the *"how."*

The real key is getting past the mental barriers, the ideas and beliefs about what meditation *"should be."* The following are internal barriers that you may experience within you and *"Ascension Mantras"* to help you shift your mindset when you find yourself off-track.

Meditation Barrier #1: I'm afraid I won't do it right. Ascension Mantra: My practice, my rules.

Like most people who start meditation I wondered if I was *"doing it right."* I created my own little mantra that I use whenever I teach meditation to others.

"My practice, my rules."

Whenever you notice you are in judgment of yourself in your practice, use that mantra. There is no right or wrong way to do it. If you're getting what you need, if you feel you're expanding in love, kindness, forgiveness, creativity, passion, awareness – or anything that you want to feel more of, you're doing it exactly right – **FOR YOU**!

Meditation Barrier #2: I don't have enough time. Ascension Mantra: Slow down, to speed up.

Think about the moments you miss because you're not fully present. Think about the time you spend worrying, paralyzed by fear or anxiety, analyzing outcomes in your head. How much time time have you invested in these un-resourceful uses of your energy?

Would you rather spend your time, going through the motions of life – or live your time more present, aware, joyful and in alignment with the emotions of your choice?

If you choose the latter, set your alarm for a little earlier tomorrow morning. It'll be worth the investment, I promise!

Meditation Barrier #3: I can't focus.

Ascension Mantra: My thoughts provide answers from within.

Protect your meditation time for the deep stuff. The real stuff. The stuff that's important to your highest human experience and your journey as a soul in a human body.

Set the intention to only allow thoughts in that support your highest good. Trust yourself to determine what thoughts need to be refocused and what thoughts need to be examined more closely. More to come on this in later chapters.

Meditation Barrier #4: A fear of what might come up.

Ascension Mantra: How can I transform this fear to love?

Everything is energy, including your thoughts and your emotions. One of the laws of energy is that energy cannot be created nor destroyed. Think of the power that is stored up in repressed, negative emotions. When we move toward and observe our fears rather than avoiding them we are presented with an opportunity to transform our fear into love, peace, joy – or other positive emotions that can help you access the true divinity within you.

When you feel yourself moving away from a sensitive thought or an emotion, consider how you can get curious about it – observe it – rather than pushing it away. More on this in the next chapter.

Meditation Barrier #5: What about prayer? Ascension Mantra: I'm listening, God. I know you can hear me too.

Meditation is a two-way dialogue with a higher power of your own belief system. Whether we believe the conversation is with our higher self, our inner being, God, angels, guides, the Universe or something else makes no difference. The bottom line is, when we get quiet and our intentions are pure – an open conversation can occur. I don't differentiate between prayer and meditation. For me, they blend together as one.

***

Now that you've learned the basics of meditation, the keyword is practice. Don't let perfection or the *"idea"* of what it should be get in the way of starting. Choose to see meditation as a way to build your faith, feel love, and make magic within you.

EXPLORATION

- ◊ What would you like to receive, what benefits are you seeking, from your meditation practice?
- ◊ What interests you about meditation?
- ◊ In what ways have you already experienced meditation by being fully present in the moment?
- ◊ Why is it worth a couple of extra minutes per day to commit to your meditation practice?
- ◊ How will you create time and space for meditation in your life? Be specific. When might you meditate? How often? And where will you do it?

The following questions are intended to be asked following your meditation practice for the first two weeks.

- ◊ What did you feel or experience during the meditation?
- ◊ What did you see or visualize?
- ◊ What did you learn, gain or let go of?
- ◊ How do you want to choose to feel following the meditation?

◊ Are there any actions you need to commit to, following the meditation?

"The way out, is in." – Thich Nhat Hanh

CHAPTER 4

BREATHE THROUGH IT

> *"Fear is excitement without breath."*
> —Robert Heller

They probably thought that I had lost it. And maybe I had. I had a stable corporate management job with a nice income and had recently been through a series of promotions, leading to finally landing my corporate *"dream job."*

Why would I suddenly decide to give that up?

My rational mind said that quitting my job to travel abroad by myself for three months was crazy. The money. The risk of my personal safety. All the things that could go wrong. But there was a deeper calling to something I didn't understand but could not deny.

I had an unshakeable faith that this – leaving my job to become a full-time online coach – was my purpose, my destiny. In order to do it right, I had to learn a completely new profession. I made the decision to sign up for three courses in Australia. The courses were each about a month apart. I could either journey back and forth – or I could find some way to occupy my time in that part of the world.

As I was being called forward on the journey of a lifetime, I was also starting to feel restless in my old life. The belongings I had once treasured suddenly began to feel suffocating. The clothes and shoes in my closet were a reminder of my focus on the external and neglect for the internal. The beautiful bedroom set I had been gifted for my wedding, was a reminder of a painful divorce. Even my car, a white Mercedes, was a reminder of past dreams of climbing the corporate ladder that were slowly transforming.

The way I was feeling was a clear message. It was time to let go and allow a new season in.

And so I decided.

"Choices, babe."

I made plans to set out on a journey across the world to gather as much knowledge as I possibly could. My plan was that over course of the next three months, I would backpack through India, Thailand, Indonesia, Australia and New Zealand for three months.

I decided it was time to *"shed"* it all – everything that would tie me to my old life. I hired an estate company, donated loads and loads to local thrift stores, and gave away an entire wardrobe. The rest was packed up into my Mercedes to be transported back to North Dakota by my two amazing parents.

As one might expect, there was a mix of reactions when I told others of my plans. One of the more common or maybe more impactful to me went something like...

"Oh, you're going to go 'find yourself."

I hated the idea of thinking that I, at the age of 35, didn't know who I was. I wanted to be seen as a strong, independent, healthy, driven woman determined to help others. I was pretty strong, like most career-driven modern women. However, there was a transformation taking place, and the woman I had been for so long no longer felt like me.

On one of my morning walks, I was meditating on the name of my future business and soon-to-be blog. After dozens of names that I could feel were not right for me, this one came to came to me like a lightening bolt: *"Iron Gypsy."*

On that day, Iron Gypsy was not who I was on the outside, but it was who I've always wanted to be on a soul level. Strong, free, able to handle whatever life throws at her, doing life her way with no fear, only a deep reverence for life itself.

I said it, and I knew. The journey ahead was the path of becoming *"Iron Gypsy."*

***

On March 2, 2017, I said goodbye to the life I knew in Houston, hugged my parents at the airport, and took off across the world with only a backpack, my laptop and a burning desire to experience and become something more.

When I stepped outside the airport in Delhi, India, a new world greeted me. We began our journey to the ashram, located in Rishikesh at the base of the Himalayas. As I sat in the back of a cab, riding nearly four hours through little Indian villages alongside cattle.

And staring out at locals dressed in traditional attire, I was far away from all I had known, yet I felt closer to the *"real me"* than I ever had.

Life at the ashram was simple -- and routine. Wake up at 5 a.m. for yoga, an hour of meditation, breakfast in silence, breath practice known as pranayama, breath theory classes, lunch, more meditation, dinner, more breath theory classes, more meditation, chanting, then sleep.

We spent hours each day focused on the breath, or prana, as it's called in the traditional language of Sanskrit. Learning to slow down our breath, breathe through our nostrils and deep into our bellies. We learned alternative nostril breathing and different patterns and rhythms of breath.

At the time, it didn't make much sense. I traveled across the globe to learn how to breathe – a skill I had been doing since my first day on the planet?

Well, okay. Iron Gypsy is up for anything.

***

There I sat. Approximately ten feet from the head Swami, my classmates all seated on their meditation blankets about six feet apart. I had been meditating for months, and at this point, felt very relaxed with my eyes closed. Not today.

We were in the middle of the capstone of our training course – a day of silence. The inner voice of shame, guilt and *"not enough"* was unleashed in full force, louder than ever.

There is he is, a truly divine human. And here you are acting like a crazy woman. Shhhhh, don't think too loud. He can probably hear your thoughts.

I'm not doing it right. They're all doing it better than I am. I want to be spiritual. I'll never be spiritual. This is crazy. My butt hurts. Just sit still.

Despite the breathing, I was more unconformable than I had ever been. The ball of anxiety I had been carrying around for years was suddenly like a volcano ready to erupt at any moment. But all I could do was sit—and squirm uncomfortably, planning how I would blame it on the hard floor or my bad back if anyone inquired about my squirming.

This was just the beginning of one of the most uncomfortable nights of my life.

My accommodation at the Ashram was a humble brick cottage I shared with three other women. I was suddenly acutely aware of how this was not *"home."* As I tossed and turned throughout the night, my body would occasionally feel the rough, cold brick. The thin, hard mattress beneath me and wool blanket covering me was a far cry from the pillow top and down comforter I once knew. There in the pitch black room I was reminded how far I was from *"normal"* life. Inside of me was a dialogue of doubt, fear and regret.

What have you done? What are you doing here? How are you going to support yourself?

I tried to use something familiar – music – to provide an ounce of comfort. There weren't enough songs in my playlist to soothe the restlessness I felt in my soul. I was never so grateful to hear the gong that woke us promptly at 5 am.

When the day of silence was over, I was *"fine,"* but I don't think I was ever the same again. Something inside of me had begun to shift that night. In the same way that my physical belongings had begun to suffocate me prior to my departure, it now seemed to be my own thoughts and inner dialogue were the source of my discomfort.

After I left the ashram, I planned to spend time in Delhi. I managed to fit in a trip to the Taj Mahal and a magical day in Jaipur before it hit me. I was sick. For three straight days, I could barely leave my bed. I ventured out only once, weak and desperate, seeking supplies. I nearly passed out in the check-out line.

There I was. Alone again. Not a soul that I knew or could count on within the entire country of millions.

I felt trapped.

I was at my edge.

There was nowhere to go. Nowhere to run.

And so, I decided.

Surrender.

Surrender to the moment.

Sit with the discomfort.

"Choices, babe."

Sometimes when we don't have any other option, the most courageous and powerful thing we can do is breathe.

Breathe and be.

***

Still sick after three days, I managed to board a plane as planned and get myself to Bangkok, Thailand, the next destination on my adventure. A bed with a beautiful white fluffy comforter, a shower with fancy glass doors, a gym, a blow dryer. All the comforts of home.

Like a queen who had come home to her castle (this was as close as it got for me since I was essentially without a permanent address), I slept like never before on top of my cushy mattress, the bright city lights of Bangkok out my window.

What was that all about?

Meditation transforms the way we think, feel and see the world. Meditation is also a process of changing our brain and the way we use it. Some researchers have called meditation *"self-directed neuroplasticity,"* meaning that when we meditate we are literally rewiring our own brain!

What I had been experiencing was simply the process of transformation. The process of becoming. The process of shifting – no longer who I was, not yet who I would be.

As I write this book it's spring in Atlanta, Ga. The other night we had a terrible storm roll through – hail, tornadoes, destruction. Thunderstorms form due to unstable energy in the atmosphere. Moist, warm air meets cold, dry air and bam – you have a wicked storm. The very next morning I went out for a run around a pond near my house. I was awestruck at how calm and beautiful it was. The pond, not a single wave on it, was a perfect mirror for big puffy clouds and a perfect sunrise that looked like it had been painted by the great Creator. When are storms more common? As seasons change – as warm air meets cold air.

Our personal transformation can feel a lot like a thunderstorm at times.

The *"storms"* I was encountering in this book (Costa Rica, my divorce, my first mediation experience, India), weren't disasters or breakdowns – they were breakthroughs. I was simply in the process of ushering in another new season, evolving on my soul's journey, and had an outbreak of a thunderstorm in the process.

Three weeks at the Ashram meditating for more than two hours per day, plus all of the lifestyle differences, plus the uncertainty of what was to come in my life was enough to send me into a Category 5 Hurricane. There was the old me, my old way of thinking and being – and the new me. These energies were clashing as I made peace with my new season.

Here's the thing about this whole – soul's journey, awaking, ascension: you don't have to do it this way. You don't have to quit your job, sell all your belongings and travel to India to transform. There is no passport required for a deep and meaningful, soul-shifting journey to your authentic light.

You can simply take a few minutes each day and gradually transform who you are and how you see the world.

Considering that you have the opportunity to re-shape of your thoughts, perceptions, and how you see yourself and the world through your meditation and your focus, let's ask again...

"What do you want to feel? How do you want to grow? What are you grateful for? How do you want to give? What is your intention?"

Breathe through it

As I weathered the storms in the months to come following my experience at the Ashram, it dawned on me why the Universe had called me to spend hundreds of hours learning about breath.

Breath is the most powerful and universal tool we have for transformation and for weathering life's storms. Breath is energy. It's purification. It has the power to change our mental and emotional state in a matter of seconds.

From a scientific perspective, it's a magical process. We take oxygen in from the external environment and bring it to every cell of the body. We release carbon dioxide, the waste product of that process. The exchange of that energy takes place in the lungs. The lungs are the only organ that comes into contact with the external environment. Think about that! The bridge between internal and external.

From a spiritual perspective, the breath is a symbol of life and renewal. It's truly an act of letting go – and receiving. It's releasing the past and creating space for new energy. It's symbolic of the yin and yang – masculine and feminine -- the opposing forces that creation is based on.

If you're not familiar with those terms, yin is feminine energy symbolic of receiving, internally focused. Yang is masculine energy, externally focused. Yin and yang, or masculine and feminine, is part of the law of polarity. Start to observe it in nature and you'll understand yourself and the world around you much better. Everything has an opposite, needs an opposite, and at the same time, those opposites are not different. They are simply two sides of the same coin.

When I learned to breathe, I was really learning to find that balance —harmony within.

So breath becomes important because it allows us to release what is no longer serving us and welcome in new energy. It allows us to let go of the past and be fully present in the moment. From a physical perspective it allows us to release and fill up with the energy we need to not only survive – but thrive.

Breath has benefits beyond meditation. As I shared earlier, it's not simply about breathing in meditation. Where in life do you need to simply breathe? Breath can help you navigate in moments where you start to panic or emotions rise up. The breath anchors us in the present and stops our emotions and beliefs from spiraling.

Breath can also help us navigate the challenging storms or even seasons of life. Sometimes, life feels challenging. Life is always serving our greatest good – our highest evolution. But we never know we're in the midst of a miracle until much later. Sometimes, the best way to navigate a storm is to breathe through it.

When you don't know what else to do, breathe through it.

Transforming Emotions: Pause. Feel. Choose.

I thought the reason I resisted meditation was that I didn't want to sit still and be unproductive. That was partly true. The deeper reason was, it made me very uncomfortable to be still because I was afraid of what would happen if I let myself feel. I believed that tears, sadness, depression were weakness.

Maybe you can relate?

With our eyes closed there is nowhere to go – nowhere to run. This is our greatest opportunity to connect with our truth, when we can learn to breathe through it. When we face those emotions in meditation, we have an opportunity to transform them by shedding light, awareness, on what was previously kept in the dark. When we sit with the emotion, breathe through it, it also loses it's power over us because we realize an emotion without a reaction to it is just a feeling. There is nothing to fear.

When sad or fearful thoughts come up in meditation. Explore them. Welcome them in like a mother welcoming her college freshman home for the weekend. *"Come on in. Have a seat. Let's talk."*

When you feel a lower vibration emotion come up in meditation or in daily life, use the process to transform the energy.

Pause: Continue to breathe, and make peace with the emotion by acknowledging you are feeling something. Emotions often show us energy in our body such as physical pain or heaviness.

Feel: Get clear on the specific emotion you are feeling. Give it a word. Give yourself permission to feel it, in order to observe it.

Choose: Ask yourself if you want to keep this emotion or choose a new emotion? If the emotion is not serving you, breathe, let it go and choose a new, empowered emotion. Choose new beliefs to support that emotion.

Using Meditation to Inspire Positive Emotions

The meditation practice I introduced in this chapter is only an introduction. You've just cracked open the door to an amazing inner journey – no passport required.

With the foundation under your belt, breath + intentional focus, you can now expand to various meditations to help you breakthrough challenges and move toward feeling what you want to feel and falling back in love with life.

Included below are some ideas for inspiring your mediation practice and specific feelings you may want to release or generate. You can also find additional guided meditations at kesleytweed.com.

Mediations to Inspire Positive Emotions

If you feel: Anxious

If you want to feel: Peace

You might try: Play soft, soothing music. Light a candle, incense or use essential oils. Close your eyes and breathe. Use Pause, Feel, Choose.

If you feel: Angry, Resentful or Jealous

If you want to feel: Grateful

You might try: Close your eyes and ask, "What am I grateful for?" Visualize what you are grateful for in as much detail as possible. Feel with as much energy as you can generate.

If you feel: Restriction

If you want to feel: Freedom

You might try: Close your eyes and listen to one or more of your favorite songs. Choose music that inspires you. Allow yourself to move with it. Allow your mind to wander freely. If a negative thought comes in, choose to release it and fixate on a positive experience you have previously had or want to create.

If you feel: Alone

If you want to feel: Unconditional Love

You might try: Close your eyes, relax your body, and place your hands on your heart, feel the energy within you. Visualize colored light at the center of your chest, pink or green work well for the heart chakra. Visualize the Earth. See people that you love, or the earth as a whole. Send loving energy to others through the use of your intention and focus on sending colored light.

If you feel: Confused

If you want to feel: Clarity

You might try: Define the challenge. What is the choice to be made? Write it down in clear, succinct words in your journal. Close your eyes. Call in the higher power of your choice to guide you. Visualize each option and notice how you feel when you create each visual. Which feels most aligned with your energy? Repeat this process as needed until the choice becomes very clear.

If you feel: Depressed

If you want to feel: Empowered

You might try: Develop "I am" affirmations. Close your eyes and repeat "I am" statements as a mantra, getting very clear on how you want to feel and owning it. Remember to use the process we learned earlier in the book: Say it. See it. Feel it. Repeat it.

If you feel: Bored

If you want to feel: Expansive

You might try: Read a passage from a self-development or spiritual book. Close your eyes, and reflect on how it relates to you or your life. One of my favorite books for reflection is Deepak Chopra's "The Seven Spiritual Laws of Success." If mindset and manifesting are for you, try, "Think and Grow Rich" by Napoleon Hill.

If you feel: Restless

If you want to feel: Driven

You might try: Choose music that lifts you up. Close your eyes and envision the ideal life you'd like to create. What do you want to experience? What do you want to be, do or have? How do you want to grow? How do you want to give? Who would you need to become to create this vision? Open your eyes and write down your vision. Then set specific and measurable goals or create a vision board to achieve it. (Google vision board if you've never created one before.)

EXPLORATION

Now that we've realized the power and impact of meditation, let's journey back to a few of the critical questions we asked earlier in the book.

1. **How do you want to feel, or what do you want to learn, by the end of this book?**
2. **Is there anything specific in life you want to change or improve?**
3. **What would it mean for you to live "The Ascended Life?"**
4. **What would you like to receive, what benefits are you seeking, from your meditation practice?**
5. **What interests you about meditation?**

Continue with your daily meditation practice, experimenting with the various mediations above. After each, journal your experience using questions like the following. Trust me, you will want this later. It's worth it!

- What did you feel or experience during the meditation?
- What did you see or visualize?
- What did you learn, gain or let go of?
- How do you want to choose to feel following the meditation?
- Are there any actions you need to commit to, following the meditation?

"Meditation practice isn't about trying to throw ourselves away and become something better.

It's about befriending who we are already."

— *Pema Chödrön*

CHAPTER 5

INTUITION

> *"Intuition is seeing with the soul."*
> — *Dean Koontz*

I had never considered myself *"intuitive."* And after a failed marriage, I had created a million reasons why it was **NOT** a good idea to trust myself.

And yet, somehow, I'd ended up traveling the world and was now standing in San Diego, Ca., outside the home of a woman I had never met. It was just minutes before my Reiki Level I and **II** training were scheduled to begin. I had a feeling that what I was about to encounter would be a very important part of my journey.

Reiki. From the first time I heard the word, it spoke to me. Reiki is *"Spiritually Guided Life Force"* energy. The word Reiki is made up of two Japanese words. *"Rei,"* which is translated to spiritual wisdom and *"Ki"* or *"chi"* which is the non-physical energy of all living things.

Reiki, a Japanese form of energy healing, is based on the idea that there is an energy that flows through us and gives us life. If our *"life force energy"* is low, then we are more likely to feel sick, depressed or anxious -- and if it is high, we are energized, positive and confident.

I was going to be in San Diego for an extended period of time due to another course I had registered for and found a local teacher to maximize my time in the area. I had never met her and didn't know anyone who had. But, when I head her voice on the Reiki Radio podcast, I knew she would be my teacher.

When I met Yolanda for the first time, instantly, I knew I had made the right decision. She too, was an Aquarius and had a gentle and mystical, yet regal presence – the type of energy that says, *"I see you. I accept you. I will never judge you. Stay in your power, sister."*

Over the course of the next two days with Yolanda and my classmates, I went through deep meditations and learned how to channel Reiki energy. We learned the Reiki principles, Reiki symbols, and how to access our own intuition.

In Reiki sessions, a practitioner connects with life force energy, then is intuitively guided to the parts of the body or energy centers that need healing.

This sounded great, but clearly I was not given the *"intuitive"* gene. *"If I was intuitive, I never would have trusted…"* Five years after my divorce, I was still blaming myself.

Although many layers of healing had occurred since my divorce, I still believed that a failed marriage was a reason **NOT** to trust myself.

I also believed that God, too, was punishing me. My vision of God was a stern drill sergeant type always looking to teach a lesson – the hard way. And when I didn't behave correctly, I had to face the consequences. This God spoke a language that I didn't understand, and somewhere inside me was a belief that all my poor luck in love was a price I was paying for a broken vow.

Besides that, *"intuition"* was for people like psychics and sages. I was far from that. I was a very *"normal"* human.

Despite all the limiting beliefs, I wanted to believe what I was hearing Yolanda teach in our Reiki training —that we are all intuitive. As I often do, I drifted off into my own mind for moment, searching for evidence.

…The voice that had told me, *"Build your faith from the ground up."*

…The sense that it was a good idea to quit my job and travel the world.

…The way my inner knowing just knew Reiki was for me and that Yolanda should be my teacher.

My intuition had led me here. And now it was guiding me to let go and embrace yet another layer of healing.

It was a magical weekend, where I felt like I was held among my soul family – all leading up to a very special ceremony and initiation. The tears rolled down my cheeks as I sat quietly in my Reiki attunement. The four of us were seated in the middle of Yolanda's living room, shoulder to shoulder, eyes closed. This was the final step in our weekend Reiki course. My teacher slowly came to each of us performing the ceremony to align our energy with the sacred energy of the Reiki symbols. (Reiki uses Japanese symbols as a point of focus for practitioners, each with its own unique meaning and vibration.)

In that moment with the tears streaming down, I was surrounded by soul family and felt supported – held -- by a higher power. There was a deep knowing, stronger than I had ever felt before. Every step, every lesson, every mistake. In that moment, the inner critic became silent and I heard the voice of love – loud and clear.

"This is exactly where you are meant to be. The journey has all led up to this."

It was time to learn to trust myself. It was time to forgive myself for the mistakes I'd make, for a broken marriage and my part in that.

It was time to stop searching for love and acceptance in things outside myself -- fitness competitions, promotions, and even relationships.

It was time to turn up the volume on the voice of love that existed within me – and begin to turn down the voice of fear.

It was time to accept that I was not broken. I was becoming.

And so, I decided.

"Choices, babe."

Reiki had opened up something inside of me – my light. *"Light"* felt a lot like love. And it had been inside me all along.

***

After my Reiki attunement, my meditations started to move in a new direction. With the forgiveness I had granted to myself, I opened up to a new relationship with a higher power – a direct line of communication. This higher power sounded more like a friendly guardian angel than the stern drill sergeant of the past. Sometimes the voices spoke in words – sometimes in symbols, sensations or my imagination.

Moments after sitting down with my eyes closed, images would come flowing in faster than I could process them. Previously, I would have thought this was just distraction. But as I learned in my Reiki training, this was my intuition. Each image held a message, but the messages came in symbols rather than a literal message.

A sky of stars, was a message that I didn't have to be the brightest star in the sky, I just needed to shine in my own way.

Tree roots, a message of rooting more deeply into who I really was.

A key. Always a symbol of the key to my next right step.

Life became my classroom and my meditation time was the space where I absorbed the lessons. My intuition truly became my inner magic, and my path to healing.

What is intuition?

You may have heard it referenced as the sixth sense, the inner voice, inner sensing, unconscious knowledge or instinct. Our intuition is an inner knowing without logical proof. Psychology and spirituality have some conflicting views on where this inner knowing comes from, but the bottom line is, both support its existence. There are four basic types of intuition.

- Clairaudience: Hearing. Like the inner voice I have been referencing throughout this book. e.g. *"Build your faith from the ground up."*

- Clairvoyance: Seeing. Often this happens through symbol like the stars, tree and key images that I saw in my meditations.

- Clairsentient: Gut feeling. Like the inner joy I felt when I was following my heart in the back of the cab in India.

- Claircognizance: Knowing, like when I knew it was my destiny to sell all my things and travel.

You may find that one of these is dominant for you, but you can learn to recognize and use all of your intuitive gifts. It's a matter of accepting the gift of intuition you already have within you and training it.

If we are all intuitive, why don't we always use it?

When I started to write this chapter, I conducted a highly scientific research study – an Instagram poll. Okay, not exactly statistically significant research; however, it did tell me something very important. 88 percent of respondents consider themselves intuitive. 94 percent of respondents wished they had a stronger connection with it. We know we have it. How do we use it?

We practice and release what stops us from it, which in most cases is our conditioning.

Over time, as we internalize the fact that logic is highly valued in society, we lose touch with our intuition. In school, we learn things like math, science, writing and reading. Each day, we're doing activities like consuming information, processing details, crunching numbers. We're asked questions, and the *"right"* answers are supposed to come from the material we were given to learn. When we do make intuitive leaps to correct answers, we're sometimes punished if we don't *"show the work,"* the step-by-step processes we were taught. For many of us, we turned off our intuition at a very young age.

I can remember very distinctly a pivotal moment in my life where I made the decision to go against my intuition. It was an innocent occurrence on what I recall was my first day of pre-school.

"Okay, and now we're going to do a project," my teacher said. I lit up inside. I loved projects. At home, my mother had an amazing way of honoring my creativity. Projects meant freedom to create what I wanted without any boundaries.

Then my teacher said, *"We're all going to make teddy bear color crayons."* Sounds great, right? Not to my highly independent, creative little Aquarian brain.

I found the nearest teacher and told her, *"I'm going to color a picture instead."*

"No," she said. *"Here, we all do the same activities, together. You're in pre-school now."*

My instincts were instantly triggered and the inner rebel was unleashed. Before I could stop it, the tears and tantrum began. My teacher was not pleased. That was even more uncomfortable for an empathic little soul. I felt guilty for how I had reacted, and so I caved. I made the teddy-bear-shaped color crayons with the rest of the kids. When my mother came to pick me up, she was filled in on my little tantrum. And I felt even worse that I had disappointed her.

Although I can 100 percent understand (and am even supportive of the teachers' wrangling me in), it's situations where we are asked to *"turn off"* our own instinct, our inner knowing, that lead to forgetting how to trust ourselves and honor our intuition.

There was an individual soul inside of me, seeking to express herself in a way that was completely unique to her. It took me decades to understand that's what I came here to do. I knew it. I felt it from a very early age, and yet, I hadn't learned to trust it.

If you look back on your life, maybe you can recall a similar experience? It could have been something as innocent as a *"no"* from an adult at a time when you were listening to the voice within you. And in that moment, you made the decision, *"They're right. I'm wrong."*

Now is the time to forgive, create a new story, and turn up the volume on your inner voice, your intuition and your unique magic.

How do I access my intuition?

Intuition looks different for everyone.

…The energy you feel – positive or overwhelming -- when you're around other people is your intuition speaking to you.

…Your laugher, your tears, what you notice when you look out into the world.

…The images, thoughts and emotions that come up when you have your eyes closed in meditation.

All of this can be your intuition. We all have the gift of intuition. Now let's, talk about how you can use it.

1. **Make time to practice.**

For some of us, using our intuition is completely natural, and maybe you're already doing it. However, if you want to refine and integrate it into daily life, it may require some additional practice. The best way to practice is in meditation because it allows us to turn off external influences and isolate the inner cues.

What you'll notice in time is that the more you practice in meditation, the more the intuitive gifts will become a part of your everyday existence and decision-making process.

2. **Ask yourself questions.**

As Tony Robbins likes to say, *"The quality of your life is a direct reflection of the quality of the questions you are asking yourself."* You can change your life just by developing the power to ask and answer your own questions.

This is the number one way that I learned to turn on my intuition. I write down a question or a series of questions that I have, then I close my eyes and go into deep meditation. The answers may come in various forms (seeing, hearing, feeling, knowing). They may come with your eyes closed, or you may end up intuitively writing answers. Sometimes, the answers don't come immediately but more questions may arise or the answers may come in a series of steps revealed over time.

Developing intuition is in fact, learning to trust yourself and a higher power. Sometimes, this means being patient for the answers to be revealed or it can also mean taking intermediate steps to get to where you need to go. Most of the time, we don't understand our intuitively guided choices until much later.

3. **Listen for your inner voice.**

All of us have an inner voice. Learn to tune into the voice inside of you. What questions do you ask yourself repeatedly? What do you say to yourself over and over again? What tone do you use? Do you ever find yourself *"hearing"* the projected voice of others – maybe a parent or other influential figure in your life – in your own head?

There are two voices inside of us, a big part of our journey to our magic is choosing which one to listen to. One voice comes from fear. The other comes from love. We learn to amp up the volume on the voice of love and turn down – or even eliminate – the voice of fear. We'll talk more about that a little later in this chapter, but the first step is simply awareness. What are you saying to yourself? Meditation is a great place to practice observing that.

4. **Look for symbols in dreams and meditation.**

As we've been discussing, we often misinterpret the symbols that occur in our dreams or in meditation as distraction or disruption. My favorite psychologist, who was also a mystic, Carl Jung, believed that the symbols we see in dreams actually come from our unconscious mind. They're not random. They are messages from the unconscious part of ourselves, speaking a language humans have known since the beginning of time – stories.

In meditation, if you let go and allow your imagination to run wild, you can also tap into this same energy and invite your intuition to speak to you in symbols.

To practice, close your eyes in meditation and release complete control. When impactful symbols come up, ask yourself, *"What does this mean? What could it symbolize? How does this relate to my life?"*

You can also use this same process with dreams. Keep a dream journal by your bed. Upon waking, immediately write down any portion of dreams, in particularly symbols, that you remember. In your morning practice, recall the dream and in a meditative state ask yourself the questions above. *"What does this mean? What could it symbolize? How does this relate to my life?"*

5. **Observe your emotions.**

This is what I've found to be the most rewarding and tricky part of this journey because, for those of us who do tend to be very *"feeling"* beings, trusting that our ability to feel is a gift and not a liability can be a bit of a *"clunky"* process. Every day, we are presented with millions of opportunities to see and feel pain within and around us. So how do both? Feel and survive in what can sometimes feel like a harsh world?

The keyword is *"observe."* Acknowledging the emotional trigger, being clear about what we're feeling, and putting a space between the stimulus and the response. *"Pause, Feel, Choose"* as we learned in the previous chapter, is a great tool. Begin to develop a practice of asking yourself how you're feeling. To master empathy, one must be able to feel it but not have to respond to it. It's also important to begin to differentiate the emotions of others and your own, also how different emotions feel in your body, a skill we'll be developing throughout this book.

6. **Go with your gut.**

Start small, but practice making decisions from the intuitive part of you. Rather than thinking about it, researching and solving problems with logic, trust your gut. Ask yourself questions like, *"What should I wear today?" "Which direction should I go to find a parking spot?" "Who might need a call to lift their spirits?"* Observe how things turn out over time when you use your intuition. Again, trust and know that we don't always see immediate benefits, but if you practice enough – you will certainly see how intuitive decisions always seem to work out.

7. **Ask for signs from the Higher Power of your own belief system.**

Another opportunity that I use frequently is asking for signs from the universe. For me, my sign from the Universe is three birds. When I was making my decision to leave my job and travel the world, I asked to see three birds in the sky if I was making the right decision. Day after day, I saw three birds. In fact, whenever I see three birds anywhere, I'm reminded that I'm supported by the Universe.

8. **Use tools to enhance your connection with energy and a Higher Power.**

Allow your intuition to guide you to other tools to support your connection with your inner knowing. This might include modalities such as Tarot or oracle cards, muscle testing or a pendulum, numerology -- or my favorite, astrology. Let your intuition guide you to research and begin to practice the other options mentioned. We will be exploring astrology later in this book.

How do I protect my energy?

This was the very first question I asked Yolanda. *"How do I protect my energy from other people?"* Many of us who feel deeply and are sensitive to energy and emotions have this very question. It's a gift, but like any strength, it needs to be refined over time.

If you are highly sensitive, the secret to managing your energy is to focus on what you can control — **YOU**. We cannot control other people, we can't control our environment, we can't control what is happening in the world, but we can control how we respond.

Therefore, when it comes to protecting your energy, the best defense is having a strong offence. Practice all of the tools that you are learning in this book —journaling, meditation, and the additional tools yet to come. Recognize that everyone is on their own journey. There is no good or bad, evolved or not evolved. We are all here with different lessons to learn. Focus on your journey, on staying in your magic.

Keep your vibration lifted. Focus on staying strong and empowered within yourself. Use your empathy to help others help themselves, but know that in order to help you must stay in your power. You must stay rooted in who you are – your magic. The best thing you can do is stay true to your journey, reach out with a helping hand, from higher, stable ground. Your daily practice is the key to centered in your magic.

How do I know if it's really my intuition?

The short answer is, practice. It will take some time to learn the unique ways that your intuition will speak to you. There is one critical differentiator that we all need to be aware of that was mentioned above. Inside each of us, there are two voices or opposing forces – a voice of love and a voice of fear.

Fear is an energy of safety, scarcity and control. Fear believes there isn't enough, that the world is out to get us and tries to manipulate every situation to stay safe. It feels heavy and unstable, because we're always trying, striving, doing, and protecting.

Fear asks questions like, *"What if I fail? What if I get hurt? What will they think? How can I control this situation?"*

It sounds like, *"I can't," "I'm not enough," "It's too difficult." "I should." "There's no way."*

Love is expansive. Opportunistic. Love connects and focuses on possibilities. Love feels calming, yet free within us, like a soft breeze and the sun shining on our face.

The energy of love asks questions like, *"How can I grow? How can I give? What is the opportunity here? How can I connect? How can I allow?"*

Love sounds like, *"I am." "I can." "I will." "I'll find a way." "I choose." "I was born to do this."*

Fear separates. Love connects and expands. Love see opportunities, where fear see barriers.

Practice, be patient, and enjoy the journey to your inner magic.

EXPLORATION

Use the questions below to eliminate potential blocks to your intuition.

- ◊ Can you recall any experiences where you were asked (potentially even innocently) by an authority figure to go against your own intuition? In what ways has this stopped you from listening to your inner voice? What new story can you create to forgive, trust and reclaim your inner voice?
- ◊ What do you believe about the higher power of your own belief system? Is there anything that needs to be healed within you in order to develop a more nurturing and open relationship?
- ◊ How was your intuition developed and encouraged, or potentially stifled, throughout your life?
- ◊ In what ways has trusting your intuition actually served your highest good?
- ◊ Consider the voice of *"love"* and *"fear"* inside of you. Can you give examples of what each sounds, feels or looks like in you?

In this chapter, we reviewed eight ways to access your intuition. The first two, making time to practice and asking yourself questions, are the foundation. Use the following steps as part of your daily practice to strengthen your connection with your intuition.

1. **Write down a question in your journal.**

2. **Set the intention to allow the voice of love to speak to you in a way that you will understand. Feel free to say a prayer, call in an angel or guide, or ask for guidance from the Universe in any way that feels right to you.**

3. **Close your eyes. Use your inner voice to repeat the question.**

4. **Allow your intuition to speak to you through symbols or visuals, words, emotions or a sudden insight or awareness.**

5. **If symbols are used, explore them by asking yourself, "What does this mean? What could it symbolize? How does this relate to my life?"**

6. **When you feel like you've reached a point of clarity, or if you sense that the answers will unfold in time, open your eyes and journal your experience.**

7. **Repeat this practice daily using different questions. Observe the different ways that your intuition is speaking to you in your meditation and also start to notice these same intuitive "hits" coming up in daily life.**

"A miracle is a shift in perception from fear to love."

—Marianne Williamson

CHAPTER 6

CHAKRAS AND YOUR MAGIC

> *"We are not human beings having a spiritual experience, we are spiritual beings having a human experience."*
> —Pierre Teilhard de Chardin

As I stepped onto the plane in Fargo, North Dakota, I tugged on the bracelet I had been wearing since my time in Thailand nearly six months ago. As my fingertips gently brushed the black and white string, the last black strand gave way.

I silently laughed to myself, *"Okay, Universe. That's a sign. The next chapter in my future book is beginning."*

About 16 hours after my parents hugged me goodbye, I landed in San Jose, the capital of Costa Rica, around 10 p.m. local time. The rain dotted the windows of the airplane as I glanced out to survey the surroundings.

Jaco, where I would be staying, was about 60 miles from the airport, so I had hired a driver to transport me. We attempted friendly conversation, although most was simple dialogue. Every now and then the rain would let up just enough for me to catch a glimpse of dark green tropical foliage lining the highway.

We arrived at my condo just before midnight. As we checked in at the gate, the driver became my translator. It dawned on me that of all the people in Jaco, he was my longest *"friend."* And I was quickly learning that my lack of command of the local language would be more of a challenge here than it had been in many of my previous world travels.

We lugged my Osprey backpack and suitcase up three flights of stairs to the condo I had rented. The driver left the luggage by the door, and I was officially – alone. I wasn't afraid, just very aware of my solitude. I had a deep sense this would not be the Costa Rican adventure I had envisioned.

When I came to Costa Rica, I had full intention of doing all the things you might imagine – surfing, dancing, eating great food. My intuition called me in a different direction.

As you may recall in the intro to this book, Costa Rica was a pivotal place in my journey. I experienced some of the most emotionally dark moments of my life there – but also some of the most magical.

As much as I wanted this to be an exciting time of catching waves and climbing waterfalls on a Costa Rican adventure, I had important soul-healing work to do.

Of course I also had some of the amazing adventures climbing waterfalls, meeting new friends, journeying to local beaches, surfing -- but many of my memories during that time are of early mornings spent on the meditation pillow in my living room or walking along the beach alone allowing Mother Nature to speak to my heart and cleanse my soul.

Adventures I thought I would have among the beaches and hiking the rainforest happened with my eyes closed – journeying deep into the depths of me.

To be honest, it was not easy. The locals were extremely kind, and I turned down many offers for companionship and exploration. I knew, that this was a time for solitude. More than a year prior, a Tarot reader had predicted that I would go through the *"dark night of the soul"* as part of my healing and awakening process.

This was it.

***

I woke up in my condo on the International Day of the Girl with a fire burning in my belly. A message was planted on my heart, begging me to share it.

"Ladies, we've got to learn to love ourselves. We are more than our bodies!" I proclaimed in a YouTube video to my Iron Gypsy coaching clients.

As soon as I finished, I questioned whether I was truly living my message.

Although I hadn't competed in a fitness show in almost two years, I was still fighting an internal battle to maintain the fitness competitor body that once defined me. The restrictions that I kept in place under the guise of *"health"* were exhausting. There was a constant anxiety over getting workouts in, shame around those times when I would binge and eat to the point of stuffing myself, and a body dysmorphia that caused me to believe that no matter how lean I was, I was certainly ballooning day-by-day.

I was a prisoner in my own mind and body.

I would never have allowed one of my clients to settle for that kind of personal confinement – even abuse. So why was it okay for me to punish myself this way?

When those words came out of my mouth, it was a wake-up call.

"We have to learn to love ourselves."

I had traveled around the world trying to *"learn."* I still had work to do.

As much as that wake-up call was painful, at the same time, it was liberating. A new identity was taking shape – one that could no longer be confined by my rigid lifestyle and self-defeating thoughts.

I was no longer to be defined solely by my external appearance or what I could achieve in the world. It was time to create what appeared to be a new me. In reality, I was just remembering who I was, peeling back the layers of a false self I had created or learned in an attempt to *"fit in"* in the world. It was time to let go. It was time to unlearn, release and re-create *"me."*

And so I decided.

"Choices, babe."

***

How to use this chapter

The Universe provided an opening to my magic through the restriction I felt around my body. But for each of us, we will reach our breaking point – our point of proclaiming to the Universe that we are ready to awaken – in a different way. For some it will show up in attachment to an external appearance, the role we play for our job, relationships we've outgrown, etc.

Now, it's time to align with your highest essence. Where in your life is it time to dig deeper, rise higher? To liberate yourself from old patterns, beliefs, emotions or behaviors that are no longer you – were maybe no ever you in the first place?

Where is it time to let go of a mask – a role you are playing – to connect with your heart, your soul and your light?

In the following sections you will be introduced to a tool that can be used to find liberation from old ways and build a new connection to the essence of you – chakras.

During my time in Costa Rica, self-healing through the chakras was my primary method for healing and growth.

Each journey into our chakras reveals a story and a soul lesson. With our eyes closed, we are provided with an opportunity to differentiate my beliefs, feelings and desires from external influence. As we dove deeper into the chakras, we are invited to reprogram our entire system to sort through our deeply held beliefs and determine what to keep and what to release and adopt a new way of being.

Our journey in this book will center around some important life themes; exploring these are a critical part of fully awakening your magic. However, the chakras are a deep and experiential process.

This chapter holds a deep body of knowledge and experiential processes that are designed to be meditated on over time. I recommend reading through the chapter once, then choosing 1-2 chakras you'd like to focus on. At a later time, after you've made your way through the rest of the book, I recommend coming back to this chapter to journey more deeply into all seven chakras. You'll be surprised at the information and deep healing that come through.

In addition to the text provided here, you can download an extended version of this chapter at www.kesleytweed.com for additional activities and information.

Your chakra journey is reclamation of who you were born to be. It's deep work. Healing work. Soul shifting work.

Let's get started.

***

What are chakras?

The word *"chakra"* means spinning wheel in the ancient language of Sanskrit. The concept of chakras is said to have originated in ancient yoga traditions and over time, has been Westernized. Although there are many systems that break down chakras further, many systems focus on a basic seven – root, sacral, solar plexus, heart, throat, third eye and crown. Each chakra is associated with specific locations in the body and correlates with themes in our lives.

Although there are many magical ways to work with chakras, for the sake of the voyage we will take together, think of the chakras like a journey through the fundamental elements of human life and psychology. Although your story is very different from anyone else's, there are opportunities for growth provided along every human journey. In working with the chakras through this lens, you have an opportunity for an awakening journey — ridding yourself of beliefs that no longer serve you and creating new beliefs that do.

Our journey through the charkas will combine self-development with energy healing to create a chakra experience unlike any other, aligning you with the true source of light within. In this section, I'm going to provide a view of the chakras that can take you on a journey to your ascended self. It is not intended to be a traditional, all encompassing point of view, but a method that can shine light on the deepest, most magical parts of you.

Chakras: A practical perspective

Chakras, and the themes associated with each chakra, provide a focal point for meditation and self-exploration. From a practical perspective, a journey through the chakras can help us examine and realign the beliefs we hold around some of the most important aspects our lives.

You may have heard the term, *"Your thoughts create your reality."* Whether or not you believe in, understand or even care to comprehend energy, one can see that what we focus on shapes our reality. What you hold in your mind **IS** what you you will see in the world.

Through sharing my story about my body, you can likely infer what my beliefs were: I am fat. I will never find true love because I am fat. I wish I could love myself, but that would require me being thinner. What I really want is love and this is my way of trying to love myself.

No matter where I went or what happened in the outside world, because this was *"my story,"* nothing could convince me otherwise. Because I was looking for evidence of this, this is what I found.

What beliefs are shaping your reality? What stories are you holding deep within you? It's time to retell the story of you from a new perspective.

Through exploring the chakras through this lens, holding the focal points covered under each chakra, we will set you free from the deeply held, unconscious beliefs that are holding you back from living the Ascended Life.

Chakras: A metaphysical perspective

From a metaphysical perspective, the chakras are an opportunity to realign your vibration. You may have heard the term, *"Everything is energy."* What does this mean exactly? Everything in our universe is made up of molecules in constant motion, including your thoughts. At every moment, you are emitting your own vibration, created by your thoughts. A law of energy is that like attracts like. If you think negative thoughts, you'll attract more negative into your life.

What does this mean for you?

As you do the work to shift your thoughts, you will shift your vibration, allowing your light to flow through you and show up externally in your life.

The Ascension Journey: The Magic of Chakras

The law of attraction, personal development, and new age spirituality get a bad reputation for simply inspiring positive thinking. In this section I want to challenge you to go deeper. It's not about thinking about something different or visualizing beams of light — but taking an honest look at what's really holding us back from all that we are capable of.

You are magic! It's time to deconstruct any belief that could hold you back from living like it!

We can change individual thoughts all day, but in order to create lasting change, we've got to go the source. That is where chakras take us a level deeper from transforming single thoughts, emotions or beliefs to looking at the entire structure.

When you witness a thought, challenge yourself to go deeper and get curious about where this thought comes from. What deeper belief needs to be released and recreated in order to set you free?

How to use the chakras to ascend

The best way to understand the chakras is to explore and experience them, and trust your intuition to guide you. The themes provided are only a starting place to explore the depths and the magic within you. Chakras are energy centers with specific themes associated with each, but we are all complex beings. Each chakra is part of a larger system. The locations and themes are not concrete but an opening to a connection to a larger whole. The chakra system works together to create your energy body (just like your physical organs work together to create your physical body) – and the themes carried within them interact to create the essence of you.

Set the intention to allow your intuition to guide you to the exact path that is best for your connecting with your light. Allow yourself to explore beyond the information provided below. Aligning the chakras is a continuous journey; we are always being presented with new opportunities to connect more deeply with our truth. Physical pain or heaviness can also be a sign that there is a story waiting to unfold, healing waiting to occur in this area of your energy system.

This chapter is filled with questions, activities and information to help you tap into the power of your chakras. You may choose to go on your chakra journey now, or you may wish to practice with one or two of the chakras and proceed with the rest of the book. Come back to take a deeper dive into all the chakras when you you feel called. The recommended way to *"process"* each of the chakras is as follows:

◊ Read *"The Magic of ..."* section for the chakra you will explore.

◊ Complete the *" Integration Meditation"* below for each chakra.

◊ Spend at a day to a week on each chakra completing the "Ascension Activity, and as many additional questions and activities as you feel are needed to align.

Integration Meditation

1. **Select the chakra you will focus on. -**

2. **Select one question from the "Ascended Life Questions" list, found under each chakra section to to explore in your meditation.**

3. **Call in a higher power. You may choose to call in angels, guides, God or higher power of your own understanding.**

4. **Focus your energy. Close your eyes and bring your breath and awareness the physical location of the chakra. Visualize the colored light associated with each chakra flowing in the physical area to "open" the chakra.**

5. **Hold the question in your awareness until your intuition begins to speak to you. Recall what we learned in the previous chapter about intuition. If meditation does not bring about any observations, try writing the question in your journal and allowing yourself to free-write any answers that come up.**

6. **Reconnect with the chakra and ask for continued alignment and healing. Visualize the colored light, this time flowing in perfect motion, like a wheel of light. You may also wish to close with one of the affirmations listed, or one of your own.**

7. **Open your eyes and journal your observations and any actions that need to be taken to heal or align.**

Download the full color Chakra Magic infographic at kesleytweed.com.

ROOT

Theme: Self-Worth

Areas of Life: Family of origin, money, physical environment and belongings, home, physical body

Affirmation: I am worthy. I am grateful.

Location: Base of Spine

The Magic of Your Root Chakra

The root chakra is the energy center connected to all that is physical – your physical body, home, environment, money, material belongings, and your family of origin. An aligned root chakra is necessary to enjoy our physical experience of being human.

Self-worth is key theme to explore when working with our root chakra. If we do not have a strong foundation of self-worth, we will continuously self-sabotage all pursuits to have a satisfying and beautiful life because we don't belief we are worthy of it. Your self-worth is the key to building, creating, attracting, and enjoying being a human.

Exploring your relationship with your body is also core to a healthy and aligned root chakra – and our health overall. Our body is our physical *"home,"* and the way we view our relationship with this temple is critical to the way we experience life. The body is also our primary mode of *"transportation"* as we travel through life. In the *"Activate Your Magic"* section, we will be considering opportunities to create a more positive relationship with your home, temple and vehicle —your body.

As part of aligning your root chakra, it can be helpful and necessary to consider your relationship family of origin – your roots. Many of our beliefs, in particular those around our self-worth and what we are worthy of, stem from experiences of our early childhood. What early memories are shaping your identity and what do you believe you are worthy of today? What early influences are affecting the type of life you believe you deserve? Outdated beliefs often live in our root chakra, keeping us from experiencing the amazing, abundant life (abundant in ways beyond just money) that we are capable of living. If you have trauma in your past, consider that this is a sign from the Universe that maybe it's time to truly heal by working with a trained professional if you have not already.

The questions and activities below are designed to help you uncover limiting beliefs that hold you back from feeling nourished, connected and worthy of creating a magical physical environment.

Integrate the Magic of Your Root Chakra

Choose one question, then complete the mediation outlined earlier in this chapter.

- How can I create a more nourishing and healthy relationship with my body? What does my body need from me?
- What are the core beliefs about life or myself were developed based on my family of origin? Are there beliefs I want to release and replace with a new, more empowering belief?
- What is my relationship with money? What outdated beliefs about money might be blocking abundance from flowing in?
- What does abundance mean to me? What do I need to do to open to greater abundance?
- What does safety mean to me? What makes me feel safe?
- Where do I find a sense of belonging? How can I cultivate a deeper sense of belonging?

Ascension Activity: Honor Your Temple

Commit to moving your body everyday for one week. This can be through any activity that you enjoy. As you move, pay attention to what you are thinking, feeling and experiencing.

- What do you feel as you move your body?
- Do you feel sensations or heaviness? This can be a signal for chakras that will be important for you to explore as you move through these sections.
- How does that breath, life force, feel in your body?
- What are you thinking and feeling? Pay particular attention to your self-talk. Are you speaking to yourself in a way that is loving and kind and encouraging?

Expand this activity to eating. Notice what you think, feel and experience as you're eating.

- How does the food taste?
- What physical senses are most activated?
- How do you feel as you eat it?
- What are you thinking or saying to yourself as you eat?
- How does the experience change for different foods?
- Spend some time journaling your general observations on your relationship with your body.
- What might you need to shift to live in greater alignment with your ascended self and to honor your temple?

SACRAL CHAKRA

Theme: Trust

Areas of Life: Emotions, creation and creativity, receiving/yin energy, sexuality

Physical location: Womb/area below the belly button

Affirmation: I trust.

Color: Orange

The Magic of Your Sacral Chakra

The sacral chakra provides us with a different sense of stability and its own unique light. It is the center connected with the emotions, creation, creativity, receiving or yin energy, pleasure and sexuality. Essentially, when the magic of our sacral center is in alignment, we're able to flow with life.

The sacral is connected with our emotions, creation and creativity, receiving/yin energy, sexuality. Consider all the the areas of life that are associated with our sacral center. In order to truly embrace all of these pleasures that are part of the human experience we need to learn to allow —to sit back, relax and let life happen. We must trust ourselves to fully open, connect, be vulnerable with ourselves and others – and know that it is safe to do so.

A core theme to explore in this chakra is your relationship to your sexuality. Sex is one of the most intimate acts and one of the greatest pleasures of the human experience. Unfortunately, many of us have had past experiences or beliefs that stop us from fully opening to the creative and spiritual power of sex. If this is the case for you, consider that now is the time to open up to deeper exploration or healing. This may involve working with a licensed therapist or counselor to find a new sense of freedom and enjoyment when it comes to sex.

The questions and activities below are designed to help you uncover limiting beliefs that hold you back from letting go and trusting the magic of life.

Integrate the Magic of Your Sacral Chakra

Choose one question, then complete the mediation outlined earlier in this chapter.

- ◊ In what areas of life would it benefit me to let go of control?
- ◊ What would it take for me to develop a greater sense of trust in myself?
- ◊ What emotions would I like to feel more often?
- ◊ Are there any emotions I'm afraid to feel? How might this affect or drain my energy?

- ◊ How do I feel when someone gives me something? How would I like to feel? How do I feel when I give something to another person?
- ◊ In what ways do I like to create or express my creativity? When do I feel most creative?
- ◊ In what ways do I allow myself to indulge for the sake of pure enjoyment? How can I welcome more of this into my life?
- ◊ What would it take for me to feel comfortable connecting with others on a deeper level? Are there any beliefs that may be stopping me? (This can mean conversation, physical touch, looking into another's eyes, etc.)
- ◊ Do I enjoy sex? If not, what might I need to explore within myself?

Ascension Activity: Eye Contact

There is a special magic that happens when we make eye contact. They say that the eyes are the windows to the soul, and when we look into human eyes, it's like we can see the inner light that exists in all of us.

Start with mirror work. Daily for one week, look into the mirror and simply observe – without judgment. What do you see? What can you find to love about the person staring back at you? Repeat the solar plexus affirmation to yourself or some self-affirming statement such as, *"I love you. I trust you."* You may even wish to post an affirmation your mirror to remind you of your commitment to loving and trusting the magic in you.

Next begin to increase your eye contact with strangers. Practice greeting those you pass with a smile and eye contact.

As a capstone to this sacral chakra work, practice looking into the eyes of someone you know and trust – a friend, lover or family member for at least one minute.

- ◊ What do you see? Share with one another after you've completed the experience.

SOLAR PLEXUS

Theme: Empowerment

Areas of Life: Confidence, certainty, leadership, career, goals, healthy boundaries

Physical location: Below rib cage and above belly button

Affirmation: I can. I will. I am empowered.

Color: Gold

The Magic of Your Solar Plexus Chakra

The solar plexus is the center that controls our sense of empowerment. The voice deep inside that says, *"I can do this"* and provides the internal source of energy to make things happen. The key word is *"internal."* The solar plexus is that natural, innate source of confidence and inner drive that moves you forward. One of the primary ways that our solar plexus can become unbalanced is when we rely on other people or things outside of ourselves for power, such seeking to earn approval or love.

The solar plexus is important to developing a will to flow forward in life. I say *"flow"* because an aligned solar plexus does not always mean a push. It's an internal, energetic pull to move toward what you want. The best way to stay aligned in this center is to trust the *"pull"* inside of you, rather than *"grinding"* your way to results. Feel into the difference in your own body.

A core theme to explore in this chakra is your relationship to power. What does power mean to you? What is your source of power? Are there areas of life where you are giving your power away? A telltale sign is where you catch yourself saying, *"X is making me feel/do/be."* Consider this: someone or something can **ONLY** have power over you when you surrender your own power. This chakra, when aligned, is an internal authority that requires permission or validation from no one.   Nor does it seek power over anyone else.

How aligned are you with your natural source of power? The questions and activities below are designed to help align you with that internal source of power and authority.

Integrate the Magic of Your Solar Plexus Chakra

Choose one question, then complete the mediation outlined earlier in this chapter.

◊ What motivates me?

◊ What gifts and talents have I been blessed with? Are there additional opportunities to share these with others?

◊ In what areas of my life am I a leader? What is my leadership style? What makes me an effective leader?

◊ What is my source of confidence? How can I make confidence self-generated and internal?

◊ What does empowerment mean to me? How do I feel exerting my own power or confidence? What helps me feel empowered?

◊ Is there anywhere in life I'm waiting for *"permission"* to move forward? What actions can I take?

◊ What are my current goals? How can I grow in my confidence to reach these goals?

◊ Do I feel comfortable exerting personal boundaries? Why are personal boundaries important?

Ascension Activity: Your Power Source

When we are connected to our authentic source of power, our magic, we are capable of so much more than we ever imagined. Sometimes, we have to rebuild this connection by reminding ourselves how amazing and capable we are!

When was the last time you set and achieved a meaningful goal? I mean really went for something that was meaningful to you? That is what we will do in the solar plexus activation activity. The following questions are designed to help you identify a goal that lights your inner fire, along with creating an actionable a strategy to achieve it.

1. **Create a list of potential goals.**
    - Write down what immediately comes to mind.
    - Think back to your childhood about things you always wanted to do.
    - Consider those things that you always said you would do *"one day"* when you had more time, money, etc.
    - What are the goals that would add the most value to your daily life?

2. **Eliminate "should" goals. This is where you must get REALLY, brutally honest!**
    - Cross out any goals that you *"should"* do for approval or love from others.
    - Cross out any goals that you *"should"* do because it's something that you need to fit in with society or *"make it"* in the world.
    - Cross out any goals that you *"should"* do because it's something that you were interested in or started a while back and feel obligated to finish.
    - Cross out any goals that feel more like a burden.

3. **Rank your goals on a scale of 1-10, based on the following factors**:
    - Value added to daily life.
    - Long-term value.
    - Personal growth through pursuit of the goal.
    - Emotional connection to the goal. (e.g. How will you feel when you've achieved it?)
    - Choose your #1 goal.
    - Which goal literally makes your eyes light up when you think about it?
    - Which goal would make you want to jump out of bed to work on it?
    - Which goal is completely internally motivated and is not for anyone else – only to feel your internal need and desire?

4. **Once you've selected your #1 goal, it's time to create your plan.**

- What is your why? **WHY** do you want this goal? How will pursuing it make you feel?
- What is one thing you will do everyday to commit to achieving your goal?
- What resources do you need to complete the goal? (do you need to learn anything new, change your daily schedule, etc.)
- What will you need to say *"no"* to in order to achieve your goal? This is **BIG** for our solar plexus. Heathy boundaries. Apply the common phrase, *"If it's not a hell yes, it's a hell no!"*
    a. How will you continue to evaluate your progress and readjust, not quit, if necessary?
    b. How will you celebrate or reward yourself once you've reached your goal?

This may seem like a lot of work to go through for setting a single goal. This activity is designed to help get clear on what is worth your energy. Once you have a vision of what you want to create, access that inner reservoir of limitless energy and go make magic!

HEART

Theme: Love

Areas of Life: Connection, compassion, relationships, values

Physical location: Center of chest, breast bone

Affirmations: I love you. Thank you. I am love.

Color: Green

The Magic of Your Heart Chakra

The heart chakra is a powerful center, located in the middle of the chakra system and connecting us with our ability to experience one of the greatest rewards of the human journey – love.

Think about the function of the human heart. The human heart pumps blood around the body, delivering the vital oxygen and nutrients to our entire body and removing waste.

The function of the heart chakra is much the same. The heart chakra is vital to our being. We all need love, and we've all had some experiences where we've experienced some form of heartbreak. The properly functioning heart chakra has the ability to transform our experience of love so that we can keep the good, and release what is not serving us.

An aligned heart chakra can take us from, *"if/then kind of love,"* and an unconditional, unlimited kind of love. When our heart chakra is out of alignment, we allow past experiences to taint our view and expectations of love. We limit our life force through a belief that we must rely on other people for love to come to us. A properly aligned heart becomes its own power center for love. A properly aligned heart center can also help us continuously release the perceptions and expectations around love that do not serve us.

We might imagine the heart chakra would involve our connection to other people. The most potent way to tap into the magic of the heart chakra, to start, is to focus on your relationship with you. You have the power inside of you to be a generator of love, meaning you have an oasis of love within you, accessible at all times. Through the questions and activities, you will learn how access this unlimited love supply within you and develop the unique ability to emit the energy of love at every moment.

Integrate the Magic of Your Heart Chakra

Choose one question, then complete the mediation outlined earlier in this chapter.

◊ What is my current definition of love?

◊ When I think about *"love"* what does it feel like in my body?

◊ In what ways do I give love to others?

◊ In what ways do I like to receive love from others?

◊ What do I love about myself?

◊ What do I love about my life?

◊ What do I love about my partner? Or what will I love about my next partner?

◊ What are ways that you can *"fill up with love"* when you find your love tank a little empty.

◊ Are there any past lovers that I need to let go of? How can I send this person love, even though the time for our romantic love is in the past?

◊ Is there anyone who has passed on from the physical world, causing a need for additional healing of my own heart? How can I feel this person's presence, beyond their physical form?

Ascension Activity: #LoveIsEverywhere Challenge

This activity is designed to make you a detective for sources of loving energy all around you, while also helping you see how you are a generator of love from within.

Challenge yourself to look for sources of love in your everyday life. How do you know when you've found a source of love? It's those moments that make your heart sing, your eyes light up, or you to take that internal pause and say to yourself, *"I love (it, that, him/her)."* Become a detective for love, looking for sources of love all around you.

Challenge yourself to look for loving moments in different areas of your life. What can you find to love about your partner? Your family? Your pets? Your job? Your home? Your community? The places, people and things you experience everyday? Become a love detective, seeking to find love everywhere!

When you find those moments of love, pause and breathe in the love, joy, bliss and gratitude you are experiencing. Feel the energy in your heart chakra and you may even feel your heart chakra expanding. When you feel those moments, speak to yourself or out loud whenever possible, *"I love [insert person, place, thing, etc]. I am love."*

Practice sharing these loving moments with others. Share with others what you love about them. Get comfortable inserting the *"L-word"* back into your vocabulary. In certain environments, using the word *"love"* is frowned upon. Challenge yourself and others to get comfortable speaking, experiencing and sharing a basic human need that we all have -- love.

Over time, with enough practice with aligning with the vibration of love, the feeling you get when you see something or someone you love will be locked in your field. You will see that love is everywhere, at all times, including within you!

Tag @irongypsylife and #loveiseverywhere in your Instagram posts. I'd love to see and share your experiences and beautiful, loving moments.

THROAT

Theme: Truth

Areas of Life: Communication, expression, influence

Physical location: Throat

Affirmations: I speak my truth.

Color: Blue

The Magic of Your Throat Chakra

The magic of the throat chakra is communicating with your authentic voice. The throat chakra is the messenger for the inspiration, knowledge and beliefs held in the other centers, making it the central hub for expression in the world.

Balance in this chakra is particularly important. Your authentic truth must not be held back; if you feel divinely connected and inspired to say or communicate something it's important to allow that energy to be expressed, whether in words or actions. It's also important not to force or overly express if you have not come to an authentic truth yet. Speaking words or beliefs that you do not believe or are not authentic to you can be harmful to your throat chakra. When we're aligned with the true magic that exists in this chakra, we magically speak in a way that is energetically received by the others and the Universe.

Speaking requires first, getting honest with ourselves and purifying any intentions that are not in alignment with our truth. A core theme to explore in this chakra is to consider the intention behind your words. Because our chakras are energy centers, the energy from which you are speaking is critical. We cannot control how others will receive our communication, as that's dependent on the state they are in when they receive them, their personal history and their own intention. Our responsibility is to be 100 percent authentic in what we are communicating and to hold the highest possible intention as we share. Pure, authentic communication is strong and certain, but it is not defensive.

To witness the power of this concept in your life, recall conversations that you've had that have gone particularly well, or not so well. What was the intention you were holding within you as you expressed yourself? What were you thinking and feeling as you were communicating? Notice how the intention impacts the receipt of the communication.

Pay attention to how ideas or thoughts that you would like to express feel in your throat chakra. Words and thoughts that align with your pure, authentic expression will feel smooth and light. Any concept that feels heavy or grainy in your throat chakra may not be authentically yours.

The following activities will help you align with your authentic truth. Use it to share and create light in the world around you.

Integrate the Magic of Your Throat Chakra

Choose one question, then complete the mediation outlined earlier in this chapter.

- ◊ What conversations can I recall that sounded and felt most authentic to me? What was the intention of my conversation? What made the conversation work so well?
- ◊ Are there any conversations I can recall that didn't sound like me? In what ways could I have been better aligned with my truth?
- ◊ What is my highest intention for what I want to express in this world?
- ◊ Are there any phrases that I use often, out loud or in my own head? What might this be telling me about me?
- ◊ Is there any truth within me that I'm holding back from communicating?
- ◊ Is there anything I'm communicating that doesn't feel 100 percent like me?
- ◊ When I feel unclear about my truth, in what ways do I find it?
- ◊ What does my authentic voice sound like? Feel like?
- ◊ What is my highest intention for what I communicate in the world? Consider **YOUR** intention and know that how it's received is not always in your control, but is dependent on the other person's state for receiving.

Ascension Activity: Speak Your Truth

As we think about the activation of the magic within our chakra resting in authentic communication, an important part of that transformation is focusing on how we share messages, versus how they are received. Remember, you cannot control how other people respond, only how your truth is communicated.

Practice talking to yourself. (Yes, I'm serious.) To do this, use the chakra meditation practice provided in this chapter as a guide. Call in the higher power of your own choice and understanding to guide you and ask it to come through your own voice. Hold a question or questions you'd like to explore in your awareness until your intuition begins to speak to you.

Speak your insights out loud. Allow the words to flow and observe how you do as they come through you. If at any time a heaviness or fear starts to come up, ask for clarity from you higher self or a higher power. Allow a conversation to take place that comes from the highest intentions that you hold.

Once you've completed the activity, write down any core learnings or observations in your journal. You may also wish to record the activity using the voice recorder on your phone so that you can replay what came through. This is your authentic truth, and what you hear may surprise you.

This activation activity may take you out of your comfort zone. If that's the case, it's particularly important to complete this work regularly.

THIRD EYE

Theme: Wisdom

Areas of Life: Thought, higher mind, analysis, perception

Physical location: Center of forehead

Affirmations: I see. I understand. I know.

Color: Indigo

The Magic of Your Third Eye Chakra

Everyday, we are presented with thousands of opportunities to harness the power of the third eye chakra. We analyze and process what's going on around us at every moment. In our third eye chakra, we see the world and make sense of what we are experiencing through our mental power. We create an interpretation – or perception – of the world around us.

The third eye chakra is the seat of our wisdom. Wisdom is the ability to use experience and knowledge for sound judgment. How do we increase our wisdom? You are doing it with this book. Likely, you've been exposed to new concepts, new ways of thinking and even new experiences that you had not previously considered. You may not agree with all of them, but through the act of considering them and deciding what you believe, you are growing in wisdom. In order to be *"wise,"* we must expose our mind to new concepts, apply them in our lives and determine for ourselves what is true.

Think of your mind like your cell phone. There are a variety of *"applications"* that have been installed in the past. The *"apps"* come from our family of origin, our environment, our past relationships, our social conditioning – all of our past experiences.

Just like keeping our phones up-to-date is continuous process, so is updating your mindset. That process includes continuously expanding your mind through learning, asking questions, seeking out new opportunities to evolve, taking risks, making new choices as you encounter your life each day.

So our question as we explore your third eye chakra is – when was the last time you updated your *"apps?"* And are the *"apps"* you're running still the ones that best serve you today?

The magic that exists in your third eye chakra is an opportunity to see the world and yourself from a new perspective, a higher perspective.

Integrate the magic of your third eye chakra

Choose one question, then complete the mediation outlined earlier in this chapter.

◊ How does having an open mind serve me?

◊ In what ways do I judge myself?

◊ In what ways do I judge others?

◊ What statements do I repeat in my mind? Are these statements serving my highest good?

◊ What questions do I frequently ask myself? Are these questions serving my highest good?

◊ How can I tune in more deeply to my inner wisdom?

◊ In what ways does my inner wisdom speak to me?

◊ Are there ways I can more fully open to hearing my inner wisdom?

◊ Is there a topic I'm curious that I could explore to increase my wisdom?

Ascension Activity: Open Your Eye, Open Your Mind

One of the greatest skills we can learn when it comes to developing the wisdom of our third eye is the ability to entertain different points of view, to see life from different angles and be open to different perspectives and the larger world – outside our own. In this activity, we're going to train our mind to see different perspectives.

Call to mind a culture or lifestyle that you see as different from your own. Imagine what life might be like for a person living in this part of the world, in this culture, or with this lifestyle. The more personal you can get the better. You may want to create a fictitious character to fully embrace this experience.

- What might he or she experience in a typical day?
- If this person came to spend a day in your life, how would their view of your life be different from your own?
- Despite the cultural differences, what human emotions, thoughts, fears, hopes, dreams or experiences might you share?
- How does this activity open up your own perspective on life? How do you see things more clearly in your own life, just from taking on a different point of view?
- In what other areas of your life or the world around you bring your greater wisdom?

CROWN CHAKRA

Theme: Faith

Areas of Life: Spirituality, consciousness, unity, divine love, freedom, beliefs

Physical location: Top of head.

Affirmations: I believe.

Color: White

The Magic of Your Crown Chakra

The crown chakra is our connection to energy from a divine source. The chakra is the gateway to an inner connectedness with God, source, the universe – or the higher power of your own belief system. When we are connected to the magic of this chakra, we feel not only supported as part of the larger whole, cut from the same cloth as our Creator.

When we open and align the magic of this chakra, we form a direct relationship with this divine consciousness that goes beyond what we have learned — letting go of what we've been told and creating a direct experience – an intimate relationship with a higher power. Our crown chakra allows us to access the infinite being within us, so it's also noticing the connection of this higher power with a non-physical, timeless part of you.

Our crown chakra allows us to feel a connection to a higher power and all that is, allowing us to sense a higher purpose for our lives and the experiences we have on a day-to-day basis. When we tap into the magic of this chakra, we see nothing happens by mistake. Everything is part of a higher divine order – every moment, every person you meet, every challenge you encounter – it's all part of the magical journey that your soul is on.

When we access the infinite part of us, we realize how we are all connected. That same timeless, soulful part of you comes and will return to the same source as your neighbor across the street and the stranger you have never met. The same magic that exists in you, although expressed and molded through different preferences, personality and experiences exists in your neighbor.

How do you know? When the crown chakra is fully experienced, you feel it. And when you look into the eyes of another, you will see a reflection of you. You will see their light – and at the same time, you will see your own ascended self!

Integrate the Magic of Your Crown Chakra

Choose one question, then complete the mediation outlined earlier in this chapter.

- ◊ In what ways do I feel connected to universal life force?
- ◊ How do I feel the connection to universal life force in my body or life?
- ◊ In what ways can I feel a connection with others, that goes beyond my human relationship with them?
- ◊ How can I deepen this relationship?
- ◊ How can I more fully understand my worth in the eyes of the Creator?
- ◊ How can I see life's challenges through the eyes of the Creator?
- ◊ In what ways can I more fully connect with others and the world around me, to embrace a feeling of unity?

Ascension Activity: Light Bath

Although beliefs about religion, spirituality, the nature of the universe vary, there is one common link among them – light. According to evolving scientific thought, we are all made up of light. World religions speak of light. Good versus evil is known as the battle between light and darkness.

Light is energy. Energy is our life force. When we focus on the light, we can move beyond the conditioned part of the mind to human beliefs about who we are and where we come from, and we connect to a pure experience of this source, life force energy itself.

To explore the magic of your crown chakra, give yourself a light bath. Begin with this prayer:

The light in me returns to the divine light of source, a light of pure love and peace.

Allow yourself to sink into a meditative space. Visualize white light streaming from above you. Allow this white light to pour over your head, around your body and see it cleansing each of your chakras. Breathe in the white light, visualize it lighting up every one of your cells, paying particular attention to the areas where you sense heaviness or tension.

Once you have cleansed your body in light, visualize a stream of golden light connecting through your crown chakra to your human mind. Through this connection, invite in an experience of a higher power. Allow this higher power to speak directly to you, or simply witness your connection to it. Hold this connection for as long as it feels right to you.

Once your meditation is complete, journal the following thoughts:

- ◊ What did your experience feel like?
- ◊ How was this direct experience different from how you've thought about religion, spirituality or connection with a higher power in the past?
- ◊ What previous beliefs were reaffirmed?
- ◊ What is the name you choose to call the higher power of your own experience?
- ◊ What do you believe about this higher power?
- ◊ How are you supported by this higher power?
- ◊ In what ways does the higher power speak to you in *"normal life"* beyond prayer or meditation?

EXPLORATION

Throughout this chapter, you've been introduced to many of ways to connect with and activate the magic of your chakras. As mentioned earlier, in order to gain the most benefit from this chapter, I recommend reading through the chapter once, then choosing 1-2 chakras you'd like to focus on.

At a later time, after you've made your way through the rest of the book, I recommend coming back to this chapter to journey more deeply into all seven chakras. Take an in-depth journey. Take as long as is needed, as you may feel called to spend more than one day on each. Work through the activities, questions and any of the additional activities suggested before moving onto the next. Trust your intuition to guide you on to the next chakra. The first time through, advance in order from root to crown.

Working with the is an ongoing process that can be part of your daily meditation and life. After you've completed your initial chakra journey, incorporate a body scan into your Daily Magic Practice. The body scan will tell you if there are specific chakras that need attention. When our chakras are out of alignment, we may notice blocks or complications in the areas of life related to that chakra, or we may sense heaviness or unease in that area of the body. Additionally, your intuition may simply guide you to a specific area through calling your attention there.

If you notice a chakra that needs attention, use the meditation process, the questions and activities to realign. If you are unable to make progress within three days, contact a Reiki Master to help you. You can find information on my distant Reiki sessions at kesleytweed.com.

> *"The great solution to all human problems is individual inner transformation."*
>
> —*Vernon Howard*

CHAPTER 7

ASTROLOGY PART I:

ASCENDING WITH THE SUN, MOON AND STARS

> *"The worst loneliness is not to be comfortable with yourself."*
> — Mark Twain

Something in me felt broken. Heartbroken.

This time, it was not a relationship ending or a break-up causing the pain.

This was a cry from the soul, it came from a place so deep I no matter how hard I tried, no matter how many hour I spent meditation, therapists and coaches I saw, or Reiki sessions I did -- I couldn't get to the root of the pain.

I felt lost. Sad. Confused. Broken.

The reality of working as an entrepreneur and the paycheck that sometimes comes with starting your own business was weighing heavily upon me. On top of that, I'd had fairly quick success billing myself as a fitness coach. That no longer felt aligned with the deeper purpose I was slowly uncovering.

For as long as I can remember, starting back to the time I was a young girl watching the morning news and dreaming of one day becoming a news anchor so I could share the real stories of people making a difference in the world – I felt deeply that I was here for something meaningful.

Three questions were on a repeating loop in my mind.

Who am I?

Why am I here?

What am I missing?

I had to be missing some kind of divine message from the Universe. I had taken a leap of faith -- left my full-time job to pursue what I thought was my *"life purpose."* I was supposed to be on the path to my destiny.

And here I was, crying, literally, everyday and even more exhausted than I had been when I was working an 8-5 and training twice per day. On top of that, I was so financially broke that for the first time in my adult life I wondered how I would pay my rent. The savings I had built up from my full-time corporate job was quickly dwindling. As I watched the numbers on my bank account drop each month – the hopes and dreams I had for coaching were beginning to fade just as quickly.

Despite the inner pain, I continued to allow soul to guide me, coach and pursue my Reiki Master certification. In the winter of 2019, I found myself once again, back in a place that had provided so much spiritual growth for me -- San Diego. This time for my Master Level Reiki Training. One day during class, Yolanda shared that she had just gone to her astrologer for her annual chart overview. I had been dabbling in astrology for about six months, since my Level I and **II** training when Yolanda gave me my first astrology report.

Just as my intuition had spoken to me in the past, I knew it was time to dive deeper. I immediately booked my first professional astrology reading – hoping that some way, somehow the reading could provide insight on how I could turn my life around and lift myself out of the darkness I had been trapped in for so many months.

***

Adrienne, a Virgo, had blue and green streaks in her hair and a calm, compassionate, nurturing energy about her. Her voice was like honey and the way her observations and questions were direct, yet soothing reminded me of the earthy comfort of a hot stone massage.

As soon as we opened up the reading, Adrienne's words penetrated to the depths of my soul.

"You have an intense energy about you. You're driven and want to make things happen. In your life, it may have felt like you had something to prove. You're a hard worker. You thrive on obstacles, and with obstacles, you like it because you think – okay – now I deserve to feel accomplished. You've gotten a lot of attention for the things you've accomplished, but it doesn't matter. You're a really hard critic. Inside yourself there is always a goal to always be better, but you don't have a standard of what that excellence is. How do you relate to that?"

"Oh shit," I thought. *"She's good."*

The conversation deepened as we talked about relationships, business and my resistance to any sort of structure in my life, including my own personal moon in Capricorn. Several tissues and an hour later, mascara running down my face, and slumping shoulders -- Adrienne looked at me and asked.

"So what's the stress about?"

"I didn't like myself in the structure. I lost myself."

"You lost yourself long before that. This isn't about losing yourself. It's about finding yourself. This is about being yourself with what is and what's natural to you. No more defining or depriving...You've been resisting yourself all along. Lose yourself to you."

And that's how my love for astrology, and my journey to finding the real me through the wisdom of the Sun, Moon and stars, began.

***

A few days later, I called Adrienne and asked her to be my first astrology teacher. We began to work together on a bi-weekly basis. Astrology is like learning another language. You learn the words, the definitions, and then determine how it all fits together into a *"conversation."*

Meanwhile, I was going deep into my own chart, using the observations Adrienne had provided to begin to turn my emotional life around.

One of the signatures we had discussed in great depth was my Moon in Capricorn in the Fourth House. As you'll learn later in this chapter, our personal Moon is the sign that can show us our deepest needs, how we care for ourselves, what we need to feel emotionally stable and how we can reflect our core energy on a daily basis.

With this particular placement, it suggested that my current nomadic lifestyle may not be the best for my inner stability – in particular at this time while I had the planet Saturn calling me to make hard decisions from a place of maturity when it came to my career, home and emotions.

I had a decision to make.

Choices, babe.

I rented an apartment for three months near San Diego's Balboa Park. This would give me enough time to figure out what the next step would be. Meanwhile, I would commit to building my business – and to *"losing myself to me."*

***

What is astrology?

Astrology is an ancient system that uses the wisdom of the cosmos – the Sun, Moon, stars and other planets – to provide guidance to those of us living on earth. Astrology connects us with the Universe, itself.

It's like a divine language, a map, that can take us on a journey to the deepest parts of ourselves and our most soul-aligned path to destiny. Astrology provides an opportunity to find the magic within us and create a life of meaning.

From a technical perspective, astrology is based on the movements of the planets in space including the Sun, Moon, Mercury, Venus, Mars, Jupiter, Saturn, Uranus and Pluto with the addition of the Pluto.

Astrology's roots have been traced back as far as 4500 **BC** in Mesopotamia. In ancient times, Priests and sages tracked the movements of the planetary bodies and provided guidance to kings and royalty on how to run their kingdoms. Astrology guided everything from how to organize communities and societies, when to plant crops, whether or not to go to war and more.

How can astrology help you?

Astrology can help us shift from pain and suffering to a path of greater harmony, health, passion, abundance, purpose and meaning. Astrology is turning on the map in your iPhone for the first time and having a map and a guide to help you understand the divine language of the Universe – and your unique path in the world.

Each of us has a unique birth chart that shows the location of the Sun, Moon and Planets at the time of our birth, which Zodiac signs the planets were located in (which we will learn about in the next chapter), and how the planets were in conversation with one anther.

The birth chart is a signature of your unique energy and light that you carry with you throughout your lifetime. As time goes on, the planets continue to move throughout the sky and make connections, called aspects, to the planets in our birth chart allowing us to access and deepen particular aspects of who we are.

Astrology helps us see the divine light within us and around us. It trains our mind to see the beauty and purpose in everything. It helps us understand how our choices manifest to create our reality.

Imagine...

What if you could learn something new about you – or develop a deeper understanding of the energies present within our Universe through this study?

What if you could see yourself through a different lens, lifting you out of the *"reality"* we living in and seeing yourself through the eyes of your creator or one with source energy?

What if astrology could be a journey deeper into the essence of you? An opportunity to clearly choose how you will align with and share your divine light with the world?

What if astrology could connect you with your ascended self and guide you to a life of meaning?

How to begin – a step-by-step guide to awakening your ascended self through astrology

In this book, we will explore the primary signatures – the foundation of your birth chart – your Sun, Moon and Rising sign. I call this your Magic Triad because unlocking the story that is held in these key placements can unlock your soul's highest intentions for this lifetime – your magic.

In this chapter, we will introduce you to the language of astrology – starting with these foundational elements. In the next chapter, we'll build on this introduction by adding the zodiac signs to our exploration.

Let us begin with the *"King of the Solar System"* and your purpose – the Sun.

Your Sun Sign: Your Purpose and Driving Force

The sun is the heart of you, the source of your energy, and the primary driving force within you. The sun connects us with our soul intention. It shows us the type of experience our soul wanted to have when it *"signed up"* to come into a body – the *"plot"* for your life story.

When someone asks, *"What's your sign?"* and your response is Aries, Aquarius, Cancer, Gemini—this is most likely your Sun sign. To be more specific, from an astrological perspective, our Sun sign is the location of the sun at the time of your birth, and it's shared with those who are born around the same time period. The sun stays in a zodiac sign for approximately twenty-eight days before moving on.

Let's take a trip back to science class. What can we recall about the sun? The sun is the heart and the king of our solar system, with all other planets revolving around it. With this in mind, what can we learn about the Universe within? When we think of the sun, think about what you know about the sun in the sky. It's bright. It's warm. Life on Earth revolves around the Sun.

From an energetic perspective, the Sun in your chart is the center of your being. It's your energy. It's the way in which you shine in the world. It's your soul essence! It's what gives you life-force energy and the way you are most naturally created to *"show up"* in the world.

Your Sun is who you are here to be and the purpose you came here to live out. The Sun is life-force energy itself. If you are repressing your Sun, you will feel disconnected from yourself—but also with your place in this world. When we not only are aware of, but embody the light of our Sun, we walk in confidence, purpose and authenticity.

Questions for Connecting with Sun

- What words would you use to describe the most authentic you?
- When do you feel most alive?
- What activities are you naturally drawn to?
- What comes naturally to you?
- When you are lacking energy or feeling out of alignment, what gives you energy?
- What gives you a feeling of *"purpose?"*
- What does it mean to *"be the change you want to see in the world?"*

The Moon: Your Emotions and Needs

The Moon is the reflection of our sun and how we live out our soul essence in daily life. In its highest expression, it provides guidance for how we are to live our soul's intention, our Sun. It represents our emotions, the deepest most intimate parts of us, the influence of our mother, our home, and, what we need to feel safe and comfortable in life.

The position of the moon at the time of your birth tells us your Moon sign, a lesser known, but highly important aspect of your chart. The Moon changes signs every 2.5 days, so even people with the same sun sign have one of 12 different moon signs. The moon is extremely important because it teaches us about our inner world. The position of our moon can teach us about our inner needs and the nature of our emotions.

Because the moon is the closest planetary body to the earth, she is our closest and most engaged teacher, a guide for existing in human form. When we respect our own Moon, we receive guidance for how to exist and care for ourselves in day-to-day life. She shows us what are true needs are and helps us learn to respect but not be overcome by our emotions. The Moon can also shows our habitual nature or subconscious patterns of behavior which stand in the way of achieving our life goals.

Think of connecting with your moon like being the exact mother you need—a mother who is deeply loving and caring, and issues a healthy dose of tough love when needed. An unhealthy expression of our moon can result in allowing our emotions, fears, or clinging to comfort to control us.

When we learn to honor our moon, we feel *"at home"* in the world and within ourselves. We can feel openly while not be overcome by emotions. We are mature, self-nurturing and live in a way that respects and reflects our soul's essence.

Questions for connecting with Moon Magic

- What emotions do you feel most often?
- What do you yearn for?
- What make you feel nourished? Comfortable? At home?

- In what ways does your intuition speak to you?
- What kinds of dreams do you have repeatedly? What might this tell you about subconscious needs or desires?
- In what ways do you practice self-care?
- What was your relationship with your mother or primary female figure like?
- How would you describe the energy of the home you grew up in?
- In what ways does how you live on a daily basis reflect who you are at your core?

Rising or Ascendant Sign: Your Identity and Talents

The Rising Sign or Ascendant is the energy, on the eastern horizon at the exact moment you came into the world and took your first breath. This creates ever further room for differentiation and uniqueness, as this energy changes every two hours (which is why the specific birth time is important when calculating an astrology chart).

Think for a minute of the symbolism behind that. That first moment. That first breath. Seeing the world for the first time. You see others, they see you, but the true personality and energy behind it all is not yet known.

The rising sign is like a filter, the point of view from which you see the world, and the point of view from which the world sees you. It's like a lens. This is usually the way people see or experience your *"vibe"* upon initial meeting. It can also define your physical characteristics. If you've ever met someone who didn't seem to exhibit the signs of their sun sign upon initial meeting, likely that is because you are likely observing the energy of their rising sign.

The rising sign is also a gift in that it helps us integrate and make our way in the world. It provides a frame of reference from which to see and experience the world. It can tell us about our specialized skills and talents – or as I like to call them our *"superpowers!"*

Questions for Connecting with Rising Sign:

- What skills and talents do you have?
- What are some of the characteristics that others notice about you upon initial meeting?
- What are some unique aspects of your body or physical appearance?
- If you had a philosophy or guiding principle for your life, what would it be?

EXPLORATION

The next step in your astrology journey is to download a free birth chart, or natal chart, if you don't already have one. You can download one for free on my website like astro.com, or do a Google search for *"free astrological birth chart."* Your chart will look similar to the one below, but with the symbols in different locations. This is map is extremely unique and it's very rare to find another human with the exact same natal chart as your own.

First, locate your Sun Sign. The symbols for the Sun is this, and the Zodiac Sign where your Sun is located will be labeled on the outer ring of the chart. For example, in the chart below, the Sun is in Aquarius.

Second, locate your Moon Sign. The symbol for the Moon sign is this. Similar to the Sun, the Zodiac sign will be provided on the outside ring of the chart. In the example below, the Moon is in Capricorn.

Finally, locate your Rising Sign or Ascendant. The Ascendant Sign is the position on the chart labeled "**ASC**." In the example below, the **ASC** falls in Libra.

In the next chapter, we'll learn about the specific energy of each Zodiac Sign, the words on the outside of the wheel which represent specific energies or vibrations.

The other symbols in the chart represent the other planets and the way that those planets interact. As you progress on your astrology journey, you'll learn all about how the signatures in your chart birth, or as I like to call it a soul map, work together to make you – **YOU**! If I can be of any help to you in the process, visit my website at kesleytweed.com to learn about opportunities to work together.

> *"The Universe is not outside you. Look inside yourself; everything you want, you already are." – Rumi*

CHAPTER 8

ASTROLOGY PART II:

> *"Your path is illuminated by a road-map of stars."*
> *— Ambika Devi*

By the Fall of that year, I was back living in my home state of North Dakota. I had immersed myself in my relationship with the sky, and the North Dakota countryside was the perfect place to do it. Each morning I would start my day at sunrise with meditation and journaling based on the energy of my chart and the current energy in the sky. At night, I would wake up to the moon peeking in my bedroom window.

I always hated to see the long, warm summer days go. And that year, the change in seasons brought with it an even stronger sting. I knew, as soon as it got cold enough, I could no longer delay *"figuring out my life."* The family cabin I was living in was not equipped for a sub-zero North Dakota winter.

I hadn't gotten a new client in months. The part-time consulting gig I had picked up wasn't enough to pay the bills, and my savings was draining down by the day. As soon as the snowflakes started to fly, I would have to move out of the cabin and back into my parents' basement.

As much as I love and respect my parents and am very grateful for their willingness to take in their 30-something entrepreneur daughter, the thought of moving back in was a painful reminder of my failure. I had given up a stable income to follow my dream of being a full-time coach, and simply put, I couldn't make it. I also recalled Adrienne's words.

"Saturn is also going to transit your moon too and feels very, very heavy... Saturn comes to our moon it's also about restriction and limitation. Basic needs. Survival needs," she had said in my first session. *"Here's the good news. You know how to work with this energy."*

During that session, Adrienne has also shared a Tarot card with me. The Strength card. The Strength card from the traditional Rider-Waite Tarot features a peaceful, angelic-like woman petting a lion.

As I meditated on that card for many days. One day, a quote from Carolyn Myss came into my awareness: *"Always go with the choice that scares you the most because that is the one that is going to help you grow."*

I paused as the tears started to fall. What was I really afraid of? I thought back to who I was before this whole *"journey."* Life was a constant battle of looking outside myself for answers and valiation. I thought about the exhaustion, the confusion and the ways I restricted myself in hopes of feeling *"enough."*

Although where I was not was certainly not *"perfect,"* I was a lot close to the real me than where I started from. I was afraid that if I went back into the corporate environment I would lose my connection with my soul and with a spirit larger than me. I was terrified that I would not be strong enough to stand firm in who I was while working in a structured, high-power environment.

But deep inside, I could feel there was a reason – a soul lesson to be learned. Everything, everything happens for a reason. Saturn was asking me to face reality. I could not continue like this. I had to do something drastic to change my physical reality – all while working to maintain the inner world, the home within, I was working on. Saturn was asking me to face my deepest fear. I recalled how Adrienne has also shared with me that when we honor Saturn, when we respond to life with patience and maturity, in the end we are always rewarded.

I knew exactly what I needed to do.

Choices, babe.

Three months later, on January 2, 2019, I traded my Birkenstocks for a pair of high heels, loaded my parents Ford Escape with everything I owned at the time (which wasn't much), and headed south to Atlanta, Ga.

My iron-willed Capricorn moon and my free-spirited Aquarius gypsy soul were headed back to the corporate world.

As I sat in the corporate lobby on that first day waiting to be ushered to my new sixth floor cubicle, I glanced down at my new journal. "

"It's written in the stars," it said on the cover.

"Yes, it certainly is," I said to myself.

I didn't know why, but I could what felt like a minor detour on the path to my destiny was exactly where I was meant to be.

***

The Zodiac

Your birth chart, or horoscope, is a snapshot in time of the exact position of the planets in the *"zodiac"* at the time of your birth. The zodiac is fixed in the sky and consists of 12 signs. The signs are derived from the constellations that mark out the path on which the sun appears to travel over the course of a year from our view on earth.

The word zodiac is derived from the Greek word mean *"Circle of Animals."* The position of the planet, which shows us a specific part of our soul, shows us the nature by which that planet will express itself.

Each of the 12 zodiac signs is associated with a specific part of the sky, a specific energy and an archetype. We will explore foundational elements of each Zodiac sign in this book. An awareness of the elements of each will help you to understand the various energetic forces that make up you – and make up the forces of nature in our greater existence.

Elements and Modes

They signs fall into categories called *"Elements"* and *"Modes"* which further help us understand the qualities of the sign and how they compare and contrast.

Modes are associated with the seasons. Each season has a cardinal energy, a fixed energy and a mutable energy.

The cardinal energies are the initiators and just as these energies bring in a new season, the presence of these signs in our charts represents a take charge, initiating energy. The Cardinal zodiac signs are Aries, Capricorn, Libra and Cancer.

At the height of each season, we have a fixed energy which is associated with upholding and maintaining consistency. The presence of these energies represents an ability to remain consistent. The Fixed zodiac signs are Taurus, Leo, Scorpio and Aquarius.

As each season comes to a close, we have a mutable energy which represents the transition to the next season. These energies represent an ability to adapt, change, transform or *"pivot"* as I like to call it. The Mutable zodiac signs are Gemini, Virgo, Sagittarius and Pisces.

The signs are further broken down into elements. You may be familiar with the elements as they are used in many modalities and cultures. The elements used in Western astrology are fire, earth, air and water.

Fire is the inspiration, motivation, and driving force of the zodiac. The fire signs are Aries, Leo and Sagittarius.

Air is our intellect and communication. The air signs are Libra, Gemini and Aquarius.

Earth signs represent physical reality and the material world. The earth signs are Capricorn, Taurus and Virgo.

Water signs are connected to our emotions, intuition and creativity. The water signs are Cancer, Scorpio and Pisces.

Each mode has one sign of each element. Understanding the elements provides an easy way to understand which zodiac signs will create a natural, easy flow and which may create some friction or require intentional understanding or alignment.

For example, fire and air create a natural flow. Earth and water create a natural flow. Mixing non-complimentary elements doesn't mean that it can't work, won't work or that there will be disharmony in a relationship within you or with another – it simply means it may take more intention, consciousness and effort. Contrasting energies can often create the most dynamic and energized results.

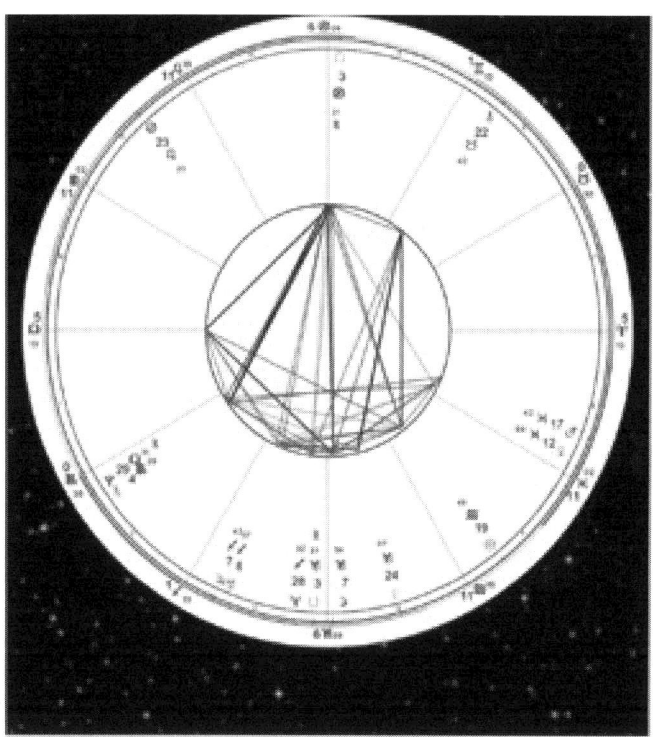

I receive many questions regarding relationship energy. Although looking at Sun signs can tell us a lot about where there may be a harmonious flow and where there will need to be more intentional effort in a relationship, I believe that any two signs **CAN** be successful in partnership. Astrology helps us cultivate awareness, acceptance and compassion for ourselves and one another. Additionally, beyond our Sun signs, there are many layers of a chart to look at when it comes to relationships, Venus, Mars, Moon, and houses such as the seventh house are critical when evaluating relationship energy.

Exploring the Universe Within You

A journey through the Zodiac is like taking a journey to the depths of you. Although your *"Magic Triad,"* your Sun, Moon and Rising sign are three core components of you – every one of the zodiac signs is present within you, those around you and you'll even see them at play in the world at large.

Before you read the following section, pull out a pen and mark the zodiac sign of your Sun, Moon and Rising Sign. Next to your *"Sun sign"* write down *"Essence, Purpose, Plot, Driving Force."* Next to the Zodiac sign representing your *"Moon Sign,"* write down *"Emotions, Needs, Comfort, Daily Life."* Next to the Zodiac sign representing your *"Rising Sign,"* write down *"Identity, Talents, Physical Appearance"*

As mentioned previously, each Zodiac sign *"rules"* over a certain aspect of your life called a *"house."* Each house is deeply complex, just as each planet and sign is as well. However, understanding these houses can bring another layer of awareness to our chart. You can locate the house of your Sun and Moon sign by looking for your Sun and Moon sign and then finding the number of the *"slice of pie"* in which each falls. For example, in the chart below, the Sun falls in the Fifth house in Aquarius and the moon falls in the Fourth House in Capricorn. The **ASC** will always fall in the first house, as it is the sign on the first house cusp.

Once you've noted the house of your Sun and Moon, also note the area of life in which each falls in your chart.

Use the reference provide a general framework for each house.

First House	Self, Appearance, Identity, Self-Actualization, Vitality
Second House	Values, Self-Worth, Resources
Third House	Communication, Mindset, Local Environment, Neighborhood, Siblings
Fourth House	Home, Family, Foundation, Inner World
Fifth House	Passions, Hobbies, Joy, Creativity, Dating Relationships, Pleasure
Sixth House	Day-to-Day Routine, Service, Health and Well-Being
Seventh House	Relationships, Partnerships, Marriage
Eighth House	Intimacy, Trust, Shadow Work, Other People's Money, Mental Health
Ninth House	Beliefs, Life Philosophy, Culture, Long-Distance Travel, Higher Learning, Publishing, Astrology
Tenth House	Career, Legacy, Goals, Public Role
Eleventh House	Social Groups, Organizations, Affiliations, Acquaintances, Community
Twelfth House	Spiritual Growth, Liberation

As you read through each of the descriptions, observe how this Zodiac sign appears within you – as well as in people you know. Each of these forces is present within you at varying degrees. Notice how the sign shows up in its highest expression and in its shadow or lower expression.

Looking at the ways the shadow shows up is a journey to living the Ascended Life! Acknowledging the presence of the shadow simply provides an opportunity to take where you are now to an even higher place!

Aries "The Ram"

- Element: Fire

- Mode: Cardinal

- Aries Magic: Courage, Determination, Drive, Motivation, Leadership, Independence, Action-Oriented, Pioneering, Autonomous, Warrior

- Soul Intention: To assert the authentic self

- Awakening Affirmation: I am brave and bold in pursuit of my best life.

- Aries Ascension: As *"the Ram,"* Aries energy connects us with an inner fire, an inner warrior, that is a great gift. To Awaken your Aries energy, put yourself in a position of leadership, where you can challenge and motivate a group. Choose a goal that lights you up inside and lights your inner fire. Goals that challenge your physical body may be particularly aligned with Aries, as once awakened, there is an unstoppable inner well of life force energy. Aim and direct the abundant source of energy within you at a meaningful target. The warrior and the light within cannot be tamed.

- Ascension Questions: What do I desire? How do I express my desires in a healthy way?

- Explore the Shadow: Because Aries is such a courageous energy, it's important to also be aware of the what might be lurking in the shadows beneath that inner fire. Explore questions like, *"What am I really afraid of? What are my insecurities?"* if you find yourself acting with impatience or anger.

Taurus "The Bull"

- Element: Earth

- Mode: Fixed

- Taurus Magic: Tenacity, Earthy, Consistency, Sensuality, Peaceful, Eye for Beauty, Stabilizing

- Soul Intention: To experience pleasure and enjoy the physical human experience

- Awakening Affirmation: I am beautiful inside and out. I am worthy of all I desire.

- Taurus Ascension: Taurus, *"the Bull,"* provides a stability and consistency that when activated, can remain steady in any situation. Taurus also reminds us that life, physical reality, is meant to be enjoyed. It's a highly sensory, physical energy in particular when it comes to touch. Taurus energy is connected to nature and from a physical perspective is naturally beautiful and has a knack for bringing beauty to the environment. Because Taurus is about physical reality, it reminds us of the importance of tending to things like our physical body, our environment and finances. The real magic of Taurus is in its ability to stay grounded in what has value, what's most important. Taurus reminds us that consistency can be magic.

- Ascension Questions: What does pleasure mean to me? How do I experience true pleasure?

- Explore the Shadow: Because a gift of Taurus is its ability to stand firm and solid in what it wants, needs and enjoys, it's important to also look at where one may be holding on too tightly. Explore questions like, *"What are my unhealthy attachments? In what ways to my attachments hold me back?"* when you feel life getting stagnant or set in your ways.

Gemini: The Twins

- Element: Air
- Mode: Mutable
- Gemini Magic: Communication, Curiosity, Playfulness, Youthful, Witty, Intelligent, Variety, Information-Seeker, Messenger
- Soul Intention: To enjoy the process of seeking information and sharing it with others.
- Awakening Affirmation: Life is fun and effortless. I constantly receive and follow divine guidance.
- Gemini Ascension: Gemini energy reminds us all to flow with it, to honor the child-like curiosity within us. As the energy of the *"Twins,"* Gemini is highly adaptable and can adapt and adjust to any situation. Gemini has a strong, fast mind and is able to absorb information, sort through what's important and share it. Where there is Gemini energy, there is a message to be brought into the world. Gemini also brings an ability to socialize and have fun. Life is your buffet! Soak it all up! Information, friends, experiences – there is no need to get stuck on anything for too long with so much in life to enjoy. Let your curiosity guide you.
- Ascension Questions: Where is my curiosity guiding me? What important message do I have to share?
- Explore the Shadow: Because Gemini has a gift and a desire for sharing information and a strong mind, it's important to ensure the mind remains calm and focused on the highest good. Explore questions like, *"In what ways does my mind hold me back? Are there areas of my life where I need to focus my energy rather than being scattered?"*

Cancer: The Crab

- Element: Water
- Mode: Cardinal
- Cancer Magic: Empathic, Comforting, Nurturing, Protective, Caring, Sensitive
- Soul Intention: To care for and nurture self and others.
- Awakening Affirmation: I take care of the world when I take care of myself.
- Cancer Ascension: Cancer energy is naturally intuitive and nurturing. Cancer is the maternal energy of the Universe that through its simple presence heels and comforts. Harness your natural ability for giving and caring for others, along with your deeply rooted sense of intuition. You can't explain it, but sometimes, *"you just know."* Trust that. Also take time to fill your own cup. Cancer energy also keeps us attached to the past and the traditions that are most meaningful to us. As the Crab, Cancer is protective of what's most important and reminds us to practice self-care and find comfort within. You owe yourself the same level of care you so freely give to others.
- Ascension Questions: In what ways does it feel good to care for others? In what ways must I also care for myself? How do my emotions guide me toward what's right?
- Explore the Shadow: Because Cancer is deeply emotional and carries deeply embedded memories, it's important to review areas where we may need to let go of the past or establish more firm boundaries. If you feel yourself overly emotional or protective, ask yourself questions like, *"Where am I holding on too tightly to the past? Where might I need to set healthy boundaries?"*

Leo: The Lion

- Element: Fire

- Mode: Fixed

- Leo Magic: Regal, Confident, Classy, Courageous, Passionate, Playful, Energetic, Charismatic, Romantic, Self-Expressive

- Soul Intention: To shine brightly, confidently share the essence of your true self and be seen.

- Awakening Affirmation: I shine so brightly that others can see their way out of the darkness.

- Awaken the Magic: Leo, the Lion, is the King of the Jungle and reminds us all that we are Kings and Queens of our own reality. Leo is the energy that is a living example of what it looks like to honor our core essence, fall in love with who we are, and express our authentic self. Leo energy is about celebration of our uniqueness and an innate passion for life, a pure and unfiltered confidence. Leo gives us permission to honor who we are and shine brightly as all of you, to be creative and to enjoy being in the spotlight. Leo reminds us to seek positions where we can lead, shine and use our natural gifts for the greater good.

- Magic Questions: What are my gifts? How can I share them in the most authentic, heartfelt and impactful way?

- Explore Your Magic: Leo energy is about authentic self-expression and although it can love applause in its purest sense, it expresses without need for applause. If you find yourself desiring attention or acting in ways that are inauthentic, ask yourself questions like, *"Where am I holding back from sharing the real me? Who would I be/do/create if no one were watching?"*

Virgo: The Virgin

- Element: Earth
- Mode: Fixed
- Virgo Magic: Honest, Giving, Helpful, Analytical, Methodical, Practical, Responsible, Self-Reliant
- Soul Intention: To serve and have purpose and meaning.
- Awakening Affirmation: I am whole, perfect, harmonious and happy.
- Virgo Ascension: Virgo, the Virgin, is an energy of purification – of making everything around it better. It has the unique ability to make even the most minor shifts for improvement of self, others and the fine details of life. Examples might include improving processes, health or virtues and character. At its core, Virgo energy is about service and helping others. It's also pure in its communication and methodical in its tactics. To awaken the Virgo energy, focus on the small but impactful gifts you have been given and how you can use them to serve others in meaningful ways.
- Ascension Questions: What small acts make me feel useful? How do I feel when I use them to help others?
- Explore the Shadow: Because Virgo is so finely tuned into how even the smallest details can result in improvements, it can have a tendency to become hyper-focused on making all things better, all of the time. If you find yourself becoming overly worried or critical, ask yourself questions like, *"Where is the pursuit of perfection getting in the way of my enjoyment? In what ways am I critical of myself that I can now release?"*

Libra: The Scales

- Element: Air
- Mode: Cardinal
- Libra Magic: Charm, Relator, Social, Optimistic, Peacemaker, Harmonious, Lover, Justice, Balanced, Fairness
- Soul Intention: To live in a beautiful state of mind.
- Awakening Affirmation: When I live in a beautiful state, everything around me becomes beautiful.
- Libra Ascension: Libra, the scales, invites us to find balance and in harmony within – and in our relationship with all things. As cardinal air, Libra energy is about creating beauty within our minds – through ideas, communication and exchange of perspective. Libra has a unique ability to see both sides of every story and act as a bridge-builder. Libra is about relationships, partnerships and connecting with things outside ourselves creating harmony, justice and balance. Libra reminds us of the importance of relationships and that all good relationships start by building harmony and beauty within.
- Ascension Questions: Where can I create greater harmony, simply by shifting my mindset? How can I create greater harmony in my relationship with myself and others?
- Explore the Shadow: Libra energy is highly relational and in its shadow will do anything to keep peace at all costs. It's important to explore questions like, *"In what unnecessary ways do I seek harmony? Are there ways I am sacrificing my own thoughts/beliefs to keep peace?"*

Scorpio: The Scorpion

- Element: Water

- Mode: Fixed

- Scorpio Magic: Powerful, Mysterious, Deep, Complex, Intuitive (Gut feelings), Passionate, Intense, Focused, Strategic, Truth-Seeker

- Soul Intention: To live with passion, intensity and seek truth.

- Awakening Affirmation: When I push myself beyond my comfort zone, I awaken my true power.

- Scorpio Ascension: Scorpio, the scorpion, reminds us to push past our own boundaries and explore the depths of ourselves and life's complexities with focus and intensity. As fixed water, Scorpio is one of the most complex and powerful energies of the zodiac. Scorpio seeks depth, truth and intimacy at all costs and intimacy and has an ability to see through the mask and find the truth. It reaches its true power when living on the edge, in a potent state of passion. Scorpio energy connects us with an instinctual intuitive and healing energy. Scorpio is strategic and highly focused with an intensity that allows it to bring light into even the darkest spaces.

- Ascension Questions: Where do I need to *"go deeper"* or transform an aspect of myself to have my inner needs met? How can I focus my intense energy and passion in the most fulfilling way?

- Explore the Shadow: Because of the power, intensity and craving of intimacy that exists in Scorpio, important questions to ask might include, *"Where do I seek power or to control others? What unmet need is this showing within me?"*

Sagittarius: The Archer

- Element: Fire
- Mode: Mutable
- Sagittarius Magic: Adventurous, Positive, Idealistic, Exuberant, Abundant, Explorer, Philosophical, Wise, Teacher/Guide
- Soul Intention: To live in a beautiful state of mind.
- Awakening Affirmation: My life is miraculous and great adventures await me!
- Sagittarius Ascension: Sagittarius, the archer, reminds us to embrace the possibilities and the adventure of life! As mutable fire, Sagittarius is an expansive and uplifting energy. It has an ability to take what is good and make it even better. This energy is also extremely wise and philosophical with an ability to see the big picture, lifting us out of the monotony of details to a place of possibility, opportunity, and optimism. Sagittarius reminds us to go with the flow, embrace the adventure of life and do it all with gratitude, generosity and joy in our hearts.
- Ascension Question: How can I live life to the fullest? What do I need to feel free? What is there an urge within me I need to explore?
- Explore the Shadow: With Sagittarius's wisdom and ability to see the big picture, it is also important to consider opportunities to shift beliefs or get practical when needed with questions like, *"Where am I holding too tightly to my own or outdated beliefs? How can I take my big ideas and break them into practical steps?"*

Capricorn: The Goat

- Element: Earth
- Mode: Cardinal
- Capricorn Magic: High Achiever, Sensible, Grit, Hard-Working, Disciplined, Successful, Authority, Maturity, Leadership, Structure, Responsible, Integrity
- Soul Intention: To endure life's challenges to reach big goals and leave a legacy.
- Awakening Affirmation: I have what it takes to conquer any challenge and reach my highest goals.
- Capricorn Ascension: Capricorn, the goat, is equipped to climb even the highest mountains! As cardinal earth, Capricorn represents an inner grit and stability – in particular when times become challenging. In fact, Capricorn thrives on conquering challenges and reminds us that we must set the bar high and then commit to the long-term journey to be successful in whatever way is meaningful to us. Capricorn asks us handle life with maturity, focus on the legacy we are here to leave and be willing to put in the hard work make our aspirations reality.
- Ascension Questions: What is a goal so big that's worth dedicating myself to it? What kind of legacy do I want to create?
- Explore the Shadow: Capricorn is always looking for a mountain to climb and is ready to push itself and those around it to the next level. It's can also be important to remember the intention behind the drive and to practice compassion with oneself and others with questions like, *"What am I really chasing? Are there ways I am being overly critical of myself or others?"*

Aquarius: The Water-Bearer

- Element: Air
- Mode: Fixed
- Aquarius Magic: Innovative, Revolutionary, Unique, Quirky, Genius, Futuristic, Unpredictable, Liberator, Individuality, Insightful
- Soul Intention: To break the status quo and create a brighter future.
- Awakening Affirmation: I exist to be the change I want to see in the world.
- Aquarius Ascension: Aquarius, the water bearer, reminds us of our authenticity and to give ourselves permission to be our quirky, cool, weird selves! Aquarius asks us to use our uniqueness to make the world a better place. As fixed air, Aquarius is connected to a vision of a utopian society where all races, classes, creeds and other *"differences"* no longer exist. Aquarius is the energy of the next phase of humanity — where all people are honored and respected for exactly who they are! Additionally, Aquarius energy is highly innovative, giving an ability to not only hold the vision but to create the systems and processes to bring what seems like far-off ideas to life!
- Ascension Question: What problems do I see in the world that I can help solve? How can I be part of the solution?
- Explore the Shadow: Because Aquarius is a highly intellectual and futuristic sign, it can detach from the present or have a challenging time connection with emotions. To stay grounded in the present and cultivate emotional awareness, it may be important to explore questions like, *"What feelings or emotions am I avoiding? Where is there room for me to be more vulnerable, intimate or emotionally connected?"*

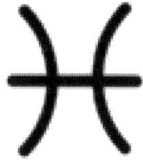

Pisces: The Fish

- Element: Water
- Mode: Mutable
- Pisces Magic: Spiritual, Mystical, Dreamy, Imaginative, Artistic, Unbounded, Expansive, Intuitive, Compassionate, Consciousness, Oneness, Healer, Empathetic
- Soul Intention: To release boundaries and merge with each moment.
- Awakening Affirmation: I flow through life with grace and ease.
- Pisces Ascension: Pisces, the fish, is an energy of flow, transcendence and oneness. As mutable water, Pisces energy is highly artistic, dreamy, intuitive and compassionate. It's not about material possession, fame or fortune. It's about merging with the moment. Being at one with yourself, your surroundings, others and source energy. Pisces is often associated with spirituality, which may be true. However, the essence of Pisces is about a feeling of connection without boundaries – a sense of losing oneself in something – living in a continuous state of a spiritual experience. Pisces invites us that life on earth is not all there is. There is a spirit soul – a magical place – within each of us. To honor Pisces, we must tap into that magic.
- Ascension Question: What makes me feel whole and at peace? What do I seek to lose myself in?
- Explore the Shadow: Because Pisces energy is highly imaginative and craves that intimacy and complete liberation from boundaries, it's important to ensure that there is strong tether to real life. For example, the shadow side of Pisces can lead to drugs, alcohol or other coping mechanism. To ensure our Pisces energy remains grounded in reality, it's important to ask questions like, *"What boundaries do I need to release or create? What is my coping mechanism?"*

How to use astrology in your daily "Alignment Practice?"

This is another point in our journey where the *"Daily Alignment Practice"* we established early in this book becomes increasingly important. Astrology is an ancient art and science – but above all it's a spiritual practice.

In the exploration, we will practice taking your new knowledge into application and finally embodiment of the essence of the signatures in your chart.

Knowledge:

The first step is to get familiar with the signatures in your chart. As discussed earlier in this chapter, you can download your free birth chart online. Contemplate how each of these signatures, in particular your Sun, Moon and Rising, show up in you. Additional research can also be helpful. There are many books, blogs and YouTube videos out there to support you. Then answer the questions below.

- What resonates with you about your astrological signature?
- What would this signature look like in it's highest vibration?
- What might this signature look like in it's lower vibration?
- How have you seen it show up in your life in the past?
- What lessons has this signature taught you?
- What gifts has this signature given you?

Application:

Now that you have a foundational understanding of your Sun, Moon and Rising, you can apply it to your life and ascension process. Consider current challenges you are facing or lessons you are learning.

- How might you be able to apply the magic of your sign to the situation?
- What might a response that's acknowledging the light of your zodiac signatures look like?
- What might a response that's connected to the shadow of your zodiac signatures look like?
- What actions might you take to stay connected to your light and ascend to your highest self?

Essence:

The application is a lot of fun because it invites us to explore more conscious responses, in alignment with our ascended self. Where this journey can take us is to a place of embodying this unique light. To some extent, you are already doing this unconsciously. What a conscious practice can do is help us to naturally show up in the highest vibration of the signatures in our chart, more often, in a more powerful way – in a way that contributes to the good of the whole.

Think about it. If your soul chose to be in a specific body, in a specific place, at a specific moment in time – you are here for a reason.

- Why might you have chosen this specific body, place, and time?
- What lessons might you be here to learn?
- What gifts might you be here to share?
- How might you be here to contribute to the good of the whole?

These are, again, deep questions that will take a lifetime to explore – that is the beauty of the journey here in *"earth school."* With the wisdom of astrology, you now have a map for your journey. When we embody and live in our magic, we are in alignment with the highest expression of the journey our soul signed up to have. We don't need to know. We go, with full faith, we are on the right path.

How does one go from application to embodiment? Practice. Sitting with the signatures in your chart. Using all of the strategies you've learned in this book to integrate them. In particular, here are two fun embodiment practices you can explore.

- Choose a song that you feel embodies your Sun, Moon and Rising Sign. Feel it. Dance to it. What does it feel like to be aligned with this energy?
- What symbols or colors come up for you when you envision your Sun, Moon and Rising Signs?

New and Full Moons

One of the best ways to begin to develop a relationship with the sky is to to track the movements of the Sun and the Moon in the sky through the moon cycle. As the Sun travels through each Zodiac sign, there will be one Full Moon and one New Moon.

On the New Moon, the Moon and the Sun are directly conjunct. The New Moon is a time where we set new intentions, and plant the seeds of what we want to manifest or understand as we begin a New Moon cycle.

New Moon activities might include:

- Gratitude journaling or meditation
- Opening to intuitive guidance for the new cycle
- Setting new intentions

- Lighting a candle to energize intentions
- Gathering with others in meditation or a sacred, joyful space
- Creating or updating your vision board

On the full moon, the moon and the sun are in direct opposition. That is why the energy is known for bringing out the crazy in the world. During this time, we are trying to find alignment between two different energies. The beautiful thing about the full moon is that the two energies, although they seem very different, are giving us an opportunity to start fresh and integrate and harmonize two opposing forces.

The Full Moon is a time of letting go. This is the time for shedding outdated beliefs or old parts of ourselves. This is a time to release.

Full Moon activities might include:

- Gratitude journaling or meditation
- Calling in guides, angels or a higher power for healing
- Using sage to cleanse your home or self
- Reiki or energy healing for energy release
- Journaling what is being released and burning the paper
- Gathering with others in a healing, sacred space or out in the moonlight
- Charging crystals in the moonlight

Although each Moon is unique, especially when working with Moon energy our intuition can guide us toward opportunities to flow with each specific energy. Trust your intuition, as the Moon is the most intuitive, receptive and nurturing of all planetary energies.

"Don't compare yourself with others. There is no comparison between the Sun and the Moon. They both shine when it's their time."

CHAPTER 9

RE-LEARNING LOVE

> *"A miracle is a shift in perception from fear to love."*
> *—A Course in Miracles*

WHEN I SAID, *"I DO,"* I had every intention of it being forever. Six years later, after counseling and a couple of years of trying to make it work, I moved across the country to Texas and started a new life – alone.

Initially, I went through the typical post-divorce protocol. Partying. Dating. And, most of all—blaming. It was his fault. And I was going to live it up, because I was a free woman, perfectly capable of finding a man to love her. I did all the things I told myself I couldn't do when I was married -- like buy a pink toaster, take trips to Europe, and go to clubs. I thought I was free and that I was open to love, but I wasn't. I was so busy pointing the finger, pretending I was a tough bitch who couldn't be hurt by any man. I continued to repeat many of the same patterns in my other relationships that I'd created in my marriage.

The same problems kept showing up.

Tears. Anger. Resentment. Blaming. Jealousy.

It was a pattern.

I had to understand this thing we call love - and was willing to do whatever it took to get there.

Love Lesson #1: Love is a choice.

On my journey around the world, I made a stop at one of the most well-known self-development events in the world - a date with destiny, held in Gold Coast, Australia. Thousands were in attendance. If healing was possible, this was the place.. The entire event was transformation – on all levels.

Then, came relationship day.

Of all the days I suited up like a *"tough girl,"* this day was the day I put more armor on than ever before. I said I wanted to forgive and heal from my previous broken relationships, but my heart felt like a two-ton safe with a padlock on it – all my negative memories and emotions stuffed inside.

I feared being hurt again more than anything in the world. I didn't trust men. I didn't trust love. And I certainly didn't trust myself.

Throughout that day, relationships were healed. Love was in the air. Tears were shed by nearly everyone in the audience as lovers rekindled their flames. And I remained stoic throughout it all. Because beneath the surface I was boiling.

At the end of a long, love-inspired day, I said to my partner for the event, *"Well that was disappointing. I had high hopes for today, but nothing. No 'breakthroughs.' I still feel as jaded as ever."* She, in her wisdom, suggested I talk to our senior team leader.

I have absolutely no idea what came out of my mouth in those moments when I began to unload the story I had been carrying for the past five years. I remember wiping my nose on my sleeves until a fellow team member brought a box of tissues. I remember the Empathetic gaze and comforting, inspiring words from my leader. I remember the genuine concern in his eyes. Beautiful words of encouragement and hope. But no transformation.

When I returned home to my lodging for the event. Standing in the large dark kitchen of the luxury home we were staying, a friend and house-mate for the week supportively probed about my experience and emotions.

I unloaded once again.

> **"Love terrifies me! I'm afraid to love. It's the thing that I want more than anything, and I'm scared to death of it because I never want to feel hurt like that again. I don't trust anyone, especially not men. I feel like every man I've loved has ripped my heart out of my chest and stomped on it. All I feel is pain."**

"Kesley, you have a choice. You can continue with these beliefs, or you can decide to tell a different story. What will you choose?"

That hit me.

Yes, I had been hurt and deceived in relationships.

That was true. But just because it's true doesn't mean it's the story I needed to keep telling myself. And behind that *"truth"* was a whole lot of bullshit and generalization – a sure sign of a *"story."*

> **When we lump all people, all men, all women, all relationships, the world or ourselves into an "always" or "never" it's definitely a tell-tale sign of a bullshit story.**
>
> **I had a choice about the story I continued to tell myself.**

My friend helped me see that telling myself the same story and reinforcing the same beliefs would create the same result. In the end, that meant ending up alone.

> **The thing I wanted the most – love – was also what I feared the most. In order to get what I wanted, I had to let go of my fear to create a new story.**

That night, thanks to the amazing men who showed care, compassion and divine masculine strength, I made a choice. I opened to love again. A journey that would take me deeper than any other.

I fully opened. I allowed myself to be vulnerable again. I began to own my true feminine nature. And in return, I was gifted with even more revelations about the nature of love.

***

Lesson #2: Love is unconditional.

I was going to be in San Diego for almost two weeks while I attended my Reiki Level I and **II** class and some additional leadership training. As the universe would have it, at complete random selection, I booked an Airbnb with a woman who shared my birthday, February 8. We became friends almost immediately. We went to yoga. We talked about astrology and holistic health. During one of our conversations, I said these words:

"I want to know everything there is to know about love."

*"Well then you **MUST** go see Dr. Lee."*

"Okay, does he have a website? I'll send him an email."

"Oh, Dr. Lee doesn't do all of that. He's the best. The smartest man I've ever met – like a love guru. But he doesn't do websites, email or social media. You'll have to call him on the phone."

After a few rounds of voicemail phone tag, we had a date.

"Well hello, Kesley. You are Teresa's friend?" Dr. Lee said with a smile, as I entered his office. He had a light-heartedness about him. Some might call him jolly – like Santa Claus without the beard, suit and belly. He invited me to sit down on the green leather couch, as he took a seat in his office chair in front of me.

"What do you want to talk about today?" (After nearly six years of working with Dr. Lee, I can tell you that he always starts his sessions in this same, non-judgmental, completely unpresumptuous way.)

"Well, I hear you are an expert on love. I've been hurt many times. I'm sick of it. I'm alone, and I want to know everything there is to know about love," I said.

And so it began.

Most of what I heard from Dr. Lee was met with a deep level of resistance within me. He told me of how our *"conditional"* ideas about love are exactly what stops us from experiencing true love. I learned about the unconditional state of mind, which is exactly as the phrase suggests. Love without any conditions, parameters or expectations.

***"Unconditional love is natural and spontaneous,"* Dr. Lee would say.**

Love that isn't earned? Isn't lost? That doesn't come with any rules or labels?

This was beyond what my mind could comprehend and triggered all of my previous wounds.

As our student/teacher relationship progressed, he began to share truths that shattered every belief I'd ever known.

Lesson #3: Love is a something we are, not something we do or receive.

"You're a romantic," he said one day with a light-hearted giggle that is one of his most endearing characteristics. (That laugher was like the spoonful of sugar to make the medicine go down.) *"I was too!"* He laughed even harder. He went on, "We grow up hearing stories about how Prince Charming will come to save us. We are taught that love is with another person. It's not your fault. It's not anyone's fault. It's just not the truth.

"You see, the truth is that we all die alone. All we have at the end of the day is the love within us. We create all these rules. All the ideas about what love is – and how it requires another person to give us something. We seek freedom – love without conditions – yet we place so many conditions around what love is."

He bursts into a song, about *"freedom."* He hums then sings, before we both burst out in laughter.

"I love that song," I say. And for the first time, I get it – what Janis Jopin really meant and what I needed to do in my life in order to experience love – real love. Unconditional love. Beyond what I had ever imagined.

"Love and do what you will," was another one of Dr. Lee's most famous lines. I began to make that statement a way of being. The feeling of freedom I felt began like a spark, a little seed. And over time, it grew into new beliefs that would heal me and set me free.

It wasn't about finding love. It was about becoming love.

All along, I thought love was something to get. What I was really looking for in another person was security. It was a feeling of *"knowing"* that, if you're here, I'm not alone. And as long as I'm not alone, it's all okay. As long as you love me, I can love myself. I was waiting for someone else to love me -- so that I could feel love within. I was waiting for someone else to confirm the way I wanted to live my life – who I wanted to be – so that I knew it was okay to **BE** that. I was waiting for someone else to set me free, to grant me permission to do life on my terms.

As I looked back on my experiences with love, specifically relationships, I realized a new purpose for the journey.

Love and relationships are my greatest teacher.

It was the pain that had brought me to this new level of freedom. I never would have gotten to this journey if it weren't for heartbreak in relationships. I never would have begun the process of seeking love from within if I'd always had that constant source that I was seeking from the outside in the form of love I wanted to receive -- romantic love.

As much as we may desire and benefit from romantic love, I need you to know the only way to find it is to start from within. What this means is that we spend time investing in our relationship with one first. We observe our inner world. We learn tools for becoming who we desire to be. We pursue our hopes and dreams. We take complete accountability for our happiness and every aspect of our lives. Imagine that you are a pie, and so is your future partner. Both partners want to have a whole pie individually, versus looking to the other for a missing piece. Once we are whole, we can receive the true gift of relationships.

We need relationships for the evolution of our soul – to ignite our magic.

Relationships provide the best opportunity for growth. The experiences and people we attract into our lives are mirrors for where we are in our journey. *"Like attracts like."*

Relationships can help us see our light. For the parts of us that we are attracted to in another often reside in us as well, we just don't see it. We need the other person to shine the light on parts of us – characteristics, interests, desires -- that were once unknown to us. Think about that. The people that you love or have loved in that past. Was there something about them that is an unclaimed part of you? Was there something in them that you were looking to *"get"* that the Universe is calling you to give to yourself?

> *What if the exact traits we loved in another, and lost, are actually traits waiting to be unlocked inside of you?*
>
> *No partner or amount of love will ever be able to fill us up – if we can't find love within first.*

Relationships can also show us the parts of ourselves that we reject – our unconscious shadow. The characteristics of others that we judge live in us too. What we project onto others, we need to explore within ourselves. For example, if we catch ourselves saying, *"He's so (negative quality),"* or *"she makes me feel (negative emotion),"* take a deeper look. How is judgment separating you from love – within and outside of you?

Assume that each relationship you've been a part of, romantic or otherwise, was a significant part of your soul's journey – the journey to reclaiming and remembering parts of your true self. The significant relationships in your mind are each a *"soul mate,"* in their own sense. Each person you connect with on an intimate level, whether they stay in your life for a short time or forever, is part of your soul's journey for a very specific reason.

The people and experiences we attract into our lives are no mistake. They are put in our lives to help us awaken our ascended self.

Only a force as powerful as love could create the type of transformation we need to reach our highest potential.

Challenges, lessons and heartbreak are not by accident. Maybe heartbreak is the Universe's way of saying, *"You're ready to progress. You're ready to ascend to a higher version of you, to love deeper than ever before."* With the greatest challenges, the deepest pain, if you really look, you will see how they ultimately led you to a higher place.

Through our relationships and, most importantly, the challenges they present, we are shown the path to our true destiny, to our true selves. Our true magic.

EXPLORATION

Reflect on the following questions:

- ◊ What relationships have been your greatest teacher?
- ◊ How have those you've loved been a mirror for you?
- ◊ Helped you reclaim or remember a lost part of you?
- ◊ Helped you discover an unmet need within yourself?

- Have there ever been ways in which you've judged others in a relationship? In what ways is that same trait in you? What did it mean to forgive and choose love?

- What is your definition of love? What does it take to feel or be in a state of love?

- What is the purpose of relationships in your life, in particular romantic or intimate relationships? What does *"relationship"* mean to you?

- Are your current definitions of love and relationships serving you, or is there an opportunity to expand or change your beliefs?

CHAPTER 10

THE REBIRTH

> *"There are two ways to live your life. One is as though nothing is a miracle. The other is as though everything is a miracle."*
> —Albert Einstein

IT CAME TO ME in the middle of a meditation, like a bolt of lightning. *"It's time to go back."*

"Go back? I don't do 'going back.' This girl moves in one direction, and that's forward," my inner critic said.

In this situation, *"going back"* was in reference to the corporate world. I had been struggling emotionally and financially for nearly a year.

Although I'd had quantum leaps in my spiritual process, externally my life felt like it was in shambles. Through the eyes of my inner critic, I was a single, late thirties, *"corporate drop-out"* living in her parent's 1960's lake cabin attempting to chase some crazy dream, with a bank account dwindling by the day.

> *"All that talk about being fearless. You're a fake. What gives you the right to guide others? You're more lost than ever!"*

The fear of *"going back"* was real.

THE REBIRTH

Fear of what others would think.

Fear of losing myself in the stress, the long hours, and work that no longer fed my soul.

Wasn't I supposed to be a free spirited-nomad who meditates, wears crystals, studies astrology and balances chakras? How could going back to the corporate world possibly be the next right step?

Post spiritual awakening, I made most decisions according to a very specific mantra. *"When faced with two decisions, go with the one that scares you the most. That is the one that will help you grow."*

One thing was certain. Going back to the corporate world scared me more than anything! My rational brain didn't quite understand it then, but my higher self and my higher power knew that there was a part of me that was yet to be reclaimed, and the only way to meet her was by *"going back."*

***

It was a dark, cold and rainy Friday night. It had been another long week at the office. I turned the lock to the door of my second story apartment, eager to get inside - and not because of the weather or the temperature. I was tired - mentally, emotionally, spiritually. I couldn't hold it together a second longer.

Instead of popping open a bottle of full-bodied Cabernet like I would normally do at this point in the week, I immediately headed to my meditation area.

I hit my knees, elbows propped up on my meditation chair, hands in a prayer position in front of me, tears rolling down my cheeks – a position I had become all too familiar with on this journey.

"Please help me," I said to the Universe.

A question popped into my head.

"Where are you investing your energy?"

More tears.

I knew exactly where I was investing my energy.

Toxic thoughts consumed me.

Resentment about why I had ended up right back where I started.

Guilt about how I wasn't living my mission.

Worry – would I ever earn the right to live my purpose again?

Desire. Why couldn't I have all that I wanted?

I'm not a math person, but if I had to do the math, I'd say approximately 99.9 percent of my thoughts were focused on things outside of my control or outside of the present.

> ***As one of my favorite teachers, Tony Robbins always says: "Where focus goes, energy flows."***

I can tell you exactly where my energy was flowing. I was consumed with thoughts of, *"Why me? What's wrong with me? Why am I such a failure? Why is this happening to me?"*

I was suffering from **VICTIM MENTALITY**.

I could preach empowerment all day. I could meditate for hours on end. It was time to **LIVE IT**! No one could save me, but **ME**!

It was time to create the **ME** I needed to be to have the life I desired.

It was time that I took control of my mind instead of allowing my inner critic to run the show.

My meditation practice and inner work once again became the launching pad for the ascended me. It became my place to claim my identity – to take a stand for the values and aspects of life that are most important to me. Because my daily environment - a cubicle in corporate America - was not what I would have considered a spiritually nourishing space, it was critical that I claimed and connected with who I was daily before entering the world.

Five days a week, I would wake up in the 4 am hour to complete my daily practice of self-reflection, journaling and meditation – followed by caring for my body with a workout -- all before my work day began.

Claiming the Ascended Me

I created a vision of the person I desired to be - my ascended self.

- What does she look like? What is her physical build? How does she dress?
- How does she move? How does she enter a room?
- What does she do to care for herself physically, mentally, emotionally and spiritually?
- What does she sound like? What is the energy of her communication, and what words does she use? What kinds of conversations does she have?

THE REBIRTH

- How does she invest her time and energy? What does she think about? What does she say to herself?
- What relationships does she invest in? Who does she enjoy spending time with?
- What does she do for fun?
- What is she learning?
- What goals and dreams does she have?
- What does she want to give to the world? What is her highest potential and purpose?
- What emotions does she experience daily?
- How would others describe her?

I created a worksheet on which I captured this information on. You can download a copy of this worksheet at: https://kesleytweed.com/the-ascended-life-worksheet/

On the first page of this worksheet, I wrote the internal world I desired to live in: My physical state, my inner dialogue, my mental focus and the emotions at the core of my being.

On the second page of this worksheet, I captured my deepest desires - as a statement of gratitude as if I had already achieved it.

Additionally, I created a vision board to bring color and additional energy to my manifestations.

Daily, I reviewed this worksheet as part of my morning meditation practice and again before going to sleep at night. I didn't just read it. I imagined it as if it were real. I visualized every detail of the experience. I felt the emotions.

Then, I would connect with the images on my vision board. This helped me further solidify the energy I needed to be in. The key to manifesting is not to wait until our manifestations come into reality to be in our desired state. In order to manifest, we must be in the energy of what we desire in the present.

When looking at my vision board, I stopped seeing something in the future, and started to experience the energy of what it would be like to have that in the present. Through that process, I aligned internally with the energy of my desired manifestations. As one of my favorite manifestation teachers Abraham-Hicks likes to say, to have what you desire, *"Feel good now!"*

Over time, day by day, I became more deeply connected with the authentic light within. I started to see a new me - and a new reality taking shape.

And because the environment wasn't a beautiful beach in Bali or Costa Rica or serene and spiritual ashram in India, I knew that the freedom, unconditional love and love for life I opened to more and more each day were not a product of my circumstances.

I was doing the deep work — the **SOUL WORK**!

I was commanding a new me to be reborn!

I was creating my ascended life!

I was claiming the ascended **ME**!

A few months after consistently adopting this process, I received a call from a friend with a lead on a consulting role - the perfect fit to allow me to have it all! More time to focus on my purpose, working from home, and the consistency I needed to continue to build my dream life!

Thank you, Universe!

And this is when I began to see that everything I believed was truth. Reality wasn't what I had been told it was. It's not about doing the work externally. Creating the life we desire is about doing the inner work.

Shift your thoughts, feelings, inner dialogue, what you focus on - and the external reality that is a vibrational match will unfold before your very eyes.

***

I awoke with jolt - a pain in my stomach like I had never felt before.

"Was it time?"

I had been preparing for this moment for nine months, but looking back I can now see it was more like a lifetime of preparation.

I waited for the cramping to pass and reached for my phone beside me.

1:17 am.

I gently tapped my mother who was sleeping beside me.

"Mom. I think it's time."

"It's time?" she responded. *"Oh wow. It's time."*

Again, I reached for my cell phone and pressed *"call"* to the first number on speed dial.

"Babe, I think it's time." Just as the words came out of my mouth, another cramp welled up inside of me.

My partner's voice was steady and calm on the other side of the line. *"Call Mama Sarahn and Djifa,"* he said.

THE REBIRTH

My partner Darin had suggested we spend the night apart for a change of energy. We were six days past the due date. As I started making *"the calls"* to the birth team, the contractions continued, already less than three minutes apart.

Within 30 minutes, my room was transformed into the dream birth sanctuary I had envisioned to bring a new life into the world - and rebirth my own. A line of candles danced along the half wall of my second story bedroom, overlooking my living room in my lofted apartment, continuing on the bathroom countertop providing gentle lighting for the entire master suite. A playlist of Trevor Hall, Rising Appalachia, Nahko and Medicine for the People and other spiritual artists provided a soothing, musical backdrop for the journey that was ahead.

Within another 30 minutes, the master suite was full of the birth team. My partner, midwife, doula, three assistants and our female black lab - Jill - all present and ready to support. My mother positioned herself downstairs, ready to pray her newest grand baby safely into the world.

The pressure of the contractions was growing more intense with each one. A combination of extreme pressure and burning. I thought back to the birthing presentation my doula had shown me. I recalled the documentaries and podcasts I had listened to. For months, I had filled my mind with every piece of information I could about how women were created to do this - to bring new life into the world.

"I was born to do this!" I said to myself.

Ooh. Another contraction.

"Just breathe through it," my doula said, as I leaned forward draping my pregnant body over the birth ball, and my partner Darin squeezed my hips.

We created a rhythmic pattern that continued for what must have been a couple of hours...

I would walk from the bed in the center of the room, into the bathroom. Dip low, hands on the bathroom countertop. Rock back and forth in squat position.

Walk back into the center of the bedroom to where my partner was standing. Place hands on the shoulders of his 6'3" muscular frame. He would hold me up as I let go of all resistance and breathed through the contraction.

"We're not going to tell you to push. When it's time, you'll know." The wisdom of my Midwife was true.

I continued the pattern for 20-30 minutes longer, as the birth team started to run the water in the tub for my dream water birth.

"I'm ready, I said."

The birth team helped me slowly lower my fatigued body into the tub. *"Now when the pressure comes, bare down and* **PUSH**,*"* my midwife instructed. Within 15 seconds, another contraction. I breathed and pushed with all my might. Within a short amount of time, another contraction. And I pushed again. The intense pressure in my stomach and lower back started to lessen. For the first time in hours, I felt...relaxed...?

"Let's get you out of the tub and get things going again," the midwife said.

Out of the tub I went. For a moment, I was frustrated. Saddened. I wondered how long my midwife would let me birth naturally before transferring me to a hospital.

"Stay focused. God, light, creator – be here with me," I silently and intently said to myself.

I breathed deeply and regained my composure.

It was in that moment I realized, I had been training my whole life for this. The meditation, the mindset work, the weight lifting, the consistent nutrition, the visualization, the hypnotherapy, the travel, the manifesting, all the books, courses and certifications.

The divorce.

The spiritual awakening and dark night of the soul.

The *"going back,"* which had landed me in Atlanta where I met my soul mate and the father of my child.

IT HAD ALL LED UP TO THIS VERY MOMENT.

I remembered the wisdom a shaman had shared with me after a sweat lodge ceremony just a couple of months earlier in Tulum, Mexico. *"When a woman goes through the birth process, a part of her dies, and a new version of her begins."*

Those words had terrified me at the time, but now I understood from a new level of consciousness.

This was my rebirth.

And I was ready.

I was born to do this. I had trained my whole life for this.

I felt a pressing on my lower tailbone. My midwife had explained that this sensation meant the baby was ready and it was time to push.

I threw off the plum-colored robe I was wearing and was ready to **GO**! This was the moment. The moment I would become a mother - and the ascended version of me.

We tried multiple positions. On a ball. On my partner's lap. Finally, I got down on all fours in the middle of my bedroom floor where I could utilize all the muscles I had worked so many years to build to **PUSH** with all my might.

"Uuuuughhhhhhhhhhh."

"She's **OUT***!"* my midwife exclaimed.

I turned around to see a beautiful little baby, the candles were still burning and at this time, the rising sun was just starting to shine through the windows.

My partner cradled me, and my mother's instinct kicked in immediately calling me to pull my newborn into my breast.

"It's a **GIRL**," the midwife said. We'd had a name picked out since the day I found out I was pregnant and had become very familiar with the feminine energy inside me. With no traditional medical intervention throughout the birth, this was the first confirmation.

We welcomed our daughter, Akasha, into the world at 8:25 am. A healthy, 7 and a half pound baby girl. And in that moment, a new me had emerged. I had ascended to a new me.

***

Every part of our journey is a deeply important part of our soul's evolution.

A marriage ending.

A dark night of the soul.

A business *"failing."*

An old me dying, as a new me and a new life were born.

As I write the final chapter of this book, I can see that those were the moments where I truly ascended.

And every single moment - every single challenge - is a pivotal and necessary part of our journey.

One of my favorite Kabbalistic teachers, Michael Berg, likes to say, *"Everything comes from the Creator, and therefore it* **MUST** *be good."*

Or put more simply in the worlds of my favorite self-development coach, Tony Robbins *"Life is* **ALWAYS** *happening for you."*

When we finally see everything that happens, every day, as a gift directly from the Creator to help us become our highest selves - we are truly on the path to ascension.

Nearly four years after I initially wrote this chapter about *"going back,"* I can look back and see how everything was leading me to exactly where I was meant to be.

"Going back," brought me to the city where I would meet a soul mate and bring new life into the world. Where I would not only birth a new child, but a new version of me.

As I wrote the final version of this chapter and the close of this book, I found a vision board I created during the heart of the ascension process I described earlier in this chapter. Nearly every item on that vision board had manifested in one form or another. I am living my own version of *"The Ascended Life,"* and allowing it to unfold according to a divine perfection each and every day!

***

We have reached an important part of your journey with this book. It's time for you too to claim your rebirth - and your ascension!

I invite you to look back. In the beginning, you made a note about where you wanted to be at the end of this book. Maybe you're not exactly where you thought you would end up, but if you allow yourself to look deeply enough, you will see something far more beautiful than the journey you had planned.

You will see the life that was meant for you. A life of twists and turns, challenges, lessons and victories. You will see a beautiful being emerging—each day—to be more and more of who you were born to be. To reveal more and more of your ascended self.

So as we close this book, I want to encourage you to claim your rebirth and your **ASCENSION**!

The ascended life isn't about creating a perfect cookie-cutter version of what you put on your vision board. It's not about forcing things or hustling.

It's about the experience of becoming the person you were always meant to be. It's about co-creating with the Universe and trusting every moment of the process.

Every step of your journey has led you to **THIS**.

You were made for this.

You were born to do this.

Claim it for yourself.

Welcome to the Ascended Life.

EXPLORATION

Spend some time reflecting on the following questions:

- ◊ Look back over your journey with this book. How have you evolved? What have you learned?

- In what ways are you grateful for the journey of your life? What specific moments, experiences or milestones have been a part of your journey - have helped you become **YOU**? What pivotal moments that didn't make sense at the time brought you to where you are now?

- What would it mean for you to claim your rebirth? Who are you committed to being going forward? How will you show up from here, forward?

- What do you visualize when you hear or read, *"The Ascended Life?"* What does that mean for you and your life? What commitments will you make to yourself to live your *"Ascended Life?"* What resources might you need to support you?

- When you hear, *"You were born to do this,"* what is the first thing that comes to mind for you? What dream is calling you?

Bringing it all Together: Claiming Your Ascended Life

Download the Ascended Life Worksheet available at:

Https://kesleytweed.com/the-ascended-life-worksheet/

On the front side, create your inner reality. On the back side, capture your vision for every aspect of your life. Write it as a statement of gratitude as if it's already come into being. Read, vision and feel the words on this worksheet at least twice daily. Create a vision board to further bring your vision and your emotional state to life.

ABOUT THE AUTHOR

KESLEY TWEED is a spiritual guide, astrologer, Reiki Master, Gallup Certified Strengths Coach, Neuro-linguistic Programming Practitioner and ascension coach.

She is a student of the Tony Robbins Leadership Mastery Programming, the co-founder of a movement called Elev8, co-host of the *"**KT** in the **DM**"* Relationship Podcast and has coached hundreds to personal transformations.

Kesley has studied with leading experts in healing the body, the mind, and soul. She's spent time in Costa Rica, New Zealand, Thailand, Bali, Australia, San Diego, Sedona, and other spiritual centers. She uses tools like astrology, Reiki energy healing, and meditation to help others journey deep within themselves to live The Ascended Life!

Learn more at kesleytweed.com or follow her on Instagram at @kesleyspiritguide.

Made in the USA
Columbia, SC
09 April 2024

3d68bec5-04c2-4da1-a54c-ed5bdc17ea46R01